Your
Angel
Is Waiting
To Help

Find her and let her touch you

Your Angel Is Waiting To Help

Find her and let her touch you

Cassandra Eason

quantum

LONDON • NEW YORK • TORONTO • SYDNEY

quantum

An imprint of W. Foulsham & Co. Ltd
The Oriel, Thames Valley Court, 183–187 Bath Road, Slough,
Berkshire SL1 4AA, England

Foulsham books can be found in all good bookshops and direct from
www.foulsham.com

ISBN 978-0-572-03492-4

Previously published as *Touched by Angels*

First published by Bokförlaget New Page AB, Sweden with the title *The Key
to Angels*. Copyright © Cassandra Eason. Published by arrangement with
Tönnheim Literary Agency, Sweden

Cover illustration by Terry Pastor based on a photograph from iStock

A CIP record for this book is available from the British Library

The moral right of the author has been asserted

Printed in Great Britain by Creative Print and Design (Wales), Ebbw Vale

Contents

The Light of Angels

Angels have been around, it is said, since the beginning of time, and represent an ancient and fundamental wisdom.

One ancient Hebrew text says that angels were made on the second day of Creation. Next, God made the animals and birds, and then he created humans so that they might be a bridge between the angels and the animals, with the potential to strive towards either state.

Angels are the ultimate shape-shifters or changers of the universe, able to appear to humans in the form to which the individual most easily relates. To some this may be as a full-blown Archangel with golden wings trailing stars, to others as a kindly stranger who helps them when they are lost or afraid, and then disappears. This is because when we are dealing with a non-physical being, we will interpret that being within our own perceptual system and our own cultural and personal understanding of angels.

Being touched by an angel is the ultimate experience, and it is this experience that I aim to help you to achieve in this book. We all have guardian angels. If you haven't met yours yet, or if you stopped believing in and talking to angels when you left childhood behind and people convinced you they weren't real, you will find in these pages not only new knowledge, but also many techniques to help you open or re-open the channels to angelic connection. If you already know and love angels, this book will provide you with ways of developing your understanding and expanding your personal angel explorations.

Whatever your starting point, I will offer you many ways of working with angelic associations – through oils, crystals, seasons, astrology and many other spiritual connections. By using these methods, I hope that you will be able to reach greater understanding of the energies of these evolved higher beings, angels and Archangels.

1

Who Are Angels?

Angels are made of pure energy that vibrates at a level we possess only in the outer, or more spiritual, layers of our aura, or personal energy field. Because of this, we see them mainly at times of prayer or meditation or when the material world suddenly fails us and we are thrown back on to our inner spiritual nature.

Angels have assumed many forms to talk to humans – from a bright beam of light to a glorious figure complete with feathered wings – and, as I have said, how we perceive angels often relates to our own understanding and culture. However, it would seem from evidence through the ages and in a variety of cultures that angels do have an existence independent of human thought or needs.

Children regularly see angels, as they do other spirit beings such as fairies. Their energy fields not yet weighed down with formal knowedge and material concerns, they operate quite naturally on this more spiritual level. However, it is possible for us as adults to get back in touch with our spiritual dimension and so more easily connect with angelic wisdom and protection by developing our understanding of the concept of energy fields and vibrations. I will help you to do this in this book.

What is not in doubt is that encounters with angelic energy forms are always transforming and positive, for angels are intermediaries between humanity and divinity. When they suddenly enter our lives – whether in dreams, visions or waking encounters – life is not the same any more, but is so much better. The experience has been likened to someone flooding a dark cave with brilliance or opening the curtain of your darkened bedroom to reveal a bright sunny morning.

This radiance may reveal how dusty some of the corners of our lives and minds are, and will open horizons so high and wide that you would need many lifetimes even to explore even a small part of them. This angelic awakening may not always be comfortable, any more than it is if someone opens those curtains on a bright morning when you were sound asleep and tells you to leave the warmth of your bed because it is a lovely day outside. But we are always glad we did go into the sunshine. It is like that with angel contact.

This book is primarily about bringing that light into your everyday world to enrich it, not about taking you away to some higher plane where people don't have to buy groceries or go to work.

Angels from around the world

Angels are described in many religions and cultures. They are traditionally found in the Judaic, Christian, Islamic and the earlier Zoroastrian fire religion. The word 'angel' comes from the Latin *angelus*, itself stemming from the Greek *aggelos*, which is a translation of the Hebrew word *mal'akh*, meaning a messenger. Angels are, in formal religion, regarded as intermediaries between God or the gods and humankind.

Over the centuries – especially in the Jewish mystical system called the Kabbalah and in medieval angelology – angels have become associated with the powers of the four elements – Earth, Air, Fire and Water; with the four directions – north, south, east and west; with the four winds; with the seven planets known to earlier astrologers; and with the 12 constellations of the zodiac. Therefore, as you work with them, you will uncover a complete spiritual system that reveals how everything fits into place and is interlinked, rather than existing in separate compartments.

The angels of the Kabbalah come from the ancient Jewish tradition, dating from the time when Israel incorporated the earlier pagan gods worshipped by the tribes of Israel and transformed them into angels serving the One True God. Some of the old gods and goddesses, especially the female ones, became demonised. We will examine this later in this book (see page 133).

Angelic lore flourished most in lands where Jewish and Christian religion transformed the former pagan gods of light into angels or saints. For example, many of the old sun gods were absorbed into the person of St Michael, Archangel of the Sun, and churches dedicated to him were built on the sites of former sun temples.

In Islam, there are four main angels: Jibril, who corresponds with the Archangel Gabriel and is the angel of revelation; Mikal, who is like Michael but is the angel of nature; Israfil, who has a wonderful voice; and Izra'il, who mirrors Azrael, the Jewish angel of death. Israfil is the angel who endows the body with its soul and heralds the Last Judgement. In Islam, angels were said to be formed from pure gems.

After the Babylonian exile (597–538 BCE), Jewish artists and writers, influenced by Mesopotamian art, gave angels wings and other specific attributes. Indeed early Christian art in Rome drew on the traditional images of winged Roman deities, such as Mercury, for inspiration. Iris, Ancient Greek goddess of the rainbow and messenger between the heavens, earth and underworld, was one of the few women elevated to angelic status. The healing functions of Mercury became transferred to Raphael who, like the god Mercury, represents the dawn.

However, it is to the fifth-century Dionysius that we owe the formalisation of the nine ranks of angels that still form the core of more formal angelology. The Judaic angels became divided into Seraphim, Cherubim, Thrones, Dominions, Powers, Virtues, Principalities, Archangels and Angels. Using invocations that included reciting the names of the Archangels – medieval magicians would seek to summon good angels into divining crystals or stones and bind them with incantations until they had revealed the information they sought about future events.

But angels were also seen in other cultures under different guises, for example the shining Devas of the Hindu faith and the Orsihas, or guardian spirits, of the Candoble faith in Brazil. The myths of the Australian Aborigines talk about different tribes of Sky Heroes, and early cave drawings depict celestial beings with antennae and haloes.

The Ancient Egyptians believed that their main gods and goddesses – Thoth, god of wisdom; Isis, the Mother, goddess of the Moon; Osiris, her consort, god of vegetation and rebirth; Horus, the sky god and son of Isis; Nephythys, the goddess of twilight; and Seth the god of storms and change – arrived from a land in the sky, later identified as the constellation Sirius B. Five and a half thousand years ago, when the rest of the world was still living in huts, these celestial beings rapidly introduced to Ancient Egypt an advanced civilisation and a sophisticated religious system.

The tall, shining opalescent beings of Celtic wisdom, who were later downgraded to fairies, have also been linked to angels, as have the original Atlanteans, whose wisdom, according to myth, was lost beneath the waves.

In the Scandinavian world were the mysterious Volsungr, a tribe of priests, healers and magicians who came from the far north after the ice age. They brought the secret of the runes and taught wisdom to these early people before disappearing northwards into the forests.

Angels and aliens

In more recent times, some angelic encounters have been described in terms of extra-terrestrial visitations from other dimensions, especially visions of the Nordics. These apparently alien beings are portrayed in ancient carvings and wall paintings of Pre-Columbian and other civilisations as golden gods from the sky. In the study of UFOs, Nordics are described as tall with blond hair, blue eyes, clear skin and oriental eyes. They are regarded as the bringers of wisdom, no less than angelic beings reinterpreted as super-galactic heroes.

Because aliens are associated with abductions, experiments and cruelty – especially by the more goblin-like greys (the smaller type of extra-terrestrial with a dome-like heads and slanting eyes, usually described as being grey and sometimes malevolent to humans) – extra-terrestrial contact is coming to be regarded less as a way of expanding our horizons and is more bound in with fears of invasion. The spirituality of the wise Nordics has been overshadowed by conspiracy theories and the stuff of science fiction.

The revival of the awareness of angels

With growing environmental awareness, Devas – higher spiritual essences that have come to be particularly associated with the natural world in the West – are a form in which spiritual essences are increasingly being experienced. I will examine this in detail in Chapter 7.

Encounters with traditional winged angels, too, are being ever more frequently reported. These angels often have haloes and wear flowing white robes. Perhaps this is a response to the gradual erosion of the natural beauty of the world by industrialisation and pollution and the fact that we seem to be moving ever further from world peace. In an increasingly commercial world, consumerism and selfishness leave unanswered our need for spiritual connection with each other and with that which is beyond ourselves. With the traditional Christian church and other formal faiths no longer answering everyone's spiritual needs, our response is to look for different ways of finding spiritual peace and a sense of belonging.

I believe that as our need for angels has grown in the modern world, so angels have responded by drawing close to many people who are searching for something beyond the material. Of course, angels never really went away, and I have collected experiences of sightings across the centuries. However, there is a new awareness of angelic forces that has resulted in angelic contact being reported in all walks of life and among those who acknowledge no formal religious faith.

Could we become angels?

Certainly the Swedish scientist, mystic and visionary Emanuel Swedenborg, who was born in Stockholm in 1688, believed we all had the potential to become angels. In his 30 large volumes, he made more than 7,000 references to angels and angelic life. His views have influenced a great deal of modern angelology, especially regarding contact with personal guardian angels.

Swedenborg believed that angels are not a divinely created, separate race but once experienced human existence and now, after physical death, live in the spiritual dimension. He taught that all people are born to become angels, whatever their religion. If they choose the path of virtue, they can continue on an angelic path after death. He said that every angel remains fully human until eternity, but in a more beautiful and perfected form; after death, these evolved angels continue to live in communities with homes, gardens and countryside, and have places of work. The only difference is that their environment is not fixed by physical or material restrictions but is created by thoughts.

A special angelic function is caring for young children who have died as they grow up in heaven. Another is helping newly deceased souls. Swedenborg said that at least two guardian angels are constantly with each individual during his or her time on earth and that a person may become aware of them in times of crisis.

They may also make contact by actively seeking to do so if this is appropriate for their and our stage of spiritual development.

Angelic voices and the wings that appear in so many paintings are, Swedenborg explained, ways of glimpsing a more perfect form of existence for those who live hard lives. Thus they might understand that it is possible to escape from the physical limitations of mortality and soar spiritually as well as physically in the next world if one takes the angelic path in life.

Though many angel experts insist that angels never were human, I am convinced we do all possess the potential to become angelic to some degree. Therefore we will work in this book on increasing our own spiritual potential in our everyday lives, for most of us can't sit around singing and playing harps!

Angels in our lives

Angels come when least expected but most needed, and the experience is always uplifting and positive. You do not need to have a doctorate in religion, to be a mystic living away from the world or even to go to church to receive angelic communication. Some people do say that angelic awareness has revolutionised their lives and caused them to become more conventionally religious. But for most of us an angelic encounter is rooted in our daily lives. It is a special moment that takes away fear or helps us to feel cared for and more able to cope with mundane problems. Angels can and do bring spirituality into the everyday world, rather than taking us away from real life. The following are four examples.

Rachel, from the Isle of Wight, had not been sleeping well and was very tired when she saw her son Thomas's angel. From when he was tiny, Thomas (a late talker) would frequently point in front of him and smile or wave at someone Rachel could not see. When he was about three, she put his bed in her own room because he would not settle alone.

> *One night, I woke and next to my son's bed I saw a spiralling light rising from what looked like a ball of light suspended in the air. The light was like a moving whisk that you use to mix eggs. It kept spinning round. The light was brilliant. I went towards the light to touch it, but as I got near the light disappeared.*

Rachel, who, like many first-time mothers, was anxious about her son, was reassured by the angelic light.

Margaret, from Plymouth, England, wrote to me through my website because her mother's angelic experience worried her.

> *I am thirty. Recently my mother had a big operation, and when I went to see her the next day, she told me she woke up in the night and saw a big angel with white wings and a golden halo smiling at her. Then Mum blinked and it was gone.*

I am really spooked. Is it the drugs or does it mean my mum is sicker than we know?

I answered:

Dear Margaret,

Relax. Your mother was very privileged. She saw her guardian angel, who was caring for her because she had had an operation and maybe was feeling scared. Sometimes when we have a crisis in our lives, we can more easily see other dimensions. Most people are not fortunate enough to see their guardian angel so clearly. Your mother is getting better and she will have her angel take care of her for many years to come. If you ask her, she may have had other psychic experiences that she has never talked about but would like to share.

Recently I heard that Margaret's mother is now well again. She told Margaret that the angel had helped her to overcome her fears. She recovered far faster than the doctors had anticipated.

In England in the 1900s, wealthy people would leave calling cards at one another's houses to say they had visited. Angels leave their calling cards all the time, as this account illustrates. This account, by Sofia, who lives in a small town in southern Sweden, shows just how ingenious angels can be at getting our attention.

In 1993, my mother, Gudrun, called Gun by her close friends, died after she contracted leukaemia. We were very close and so it was very hard after her death. Three months later, my mother's partner killed himself, as he felt he could not live without her.

The first angel appeared on the hallway floor, as a bookmark, a little angel picture. I didn't pay much attention to it at the time, though I have no idea where the picture could have come from – it just appeared out of nowhere.

One year after my mother died, I was taking plates out of the cupboard for dinner. When I took out the second row of plates, behind them was an old yellowing bookmark. When I turned it over, on the other side was written 'Av Gun' (By Gun) in my mother's handwriting. But my mother had not collected angel cards as a child.

On another occasion, I took out a crystal bowl that had belonged to my mother and her partner. In it was a card showing two angels, a boy and girl angel holding hands.

Angel bookmarks appear every now and then, when I need support. The latest was a year ago. I had separated from my husband and was feeling sad and alone. Nowadays I see them as greetings from my mother. She is still there for me when I have bad times.

I found Susan's story in some old records at the Alister Hardy Research Centre in Oxford, England, which researches and collates information about all kinds of spiritual experiences. I was for a time an Honorary Research Fellow there, and answered letters from people who wrote to the organisation seeking help or advice or just wanting to share their experiences of angelic encounters.

Susan's angel came when she was giving birth alone in a hospital in Kent, in south-east England, after she had been evacuated from London to escape the bombing during the Second World War. She writes:

> *I woke suddenly. There was a moon and it was not dark. Facing the window was the figure of a man wearing white. His head was slightly bent back as if in prayer or on sentinel duty. As I looked in astonishment the figure dissolved before my eyes, leaving a wisp of white that looked like a cloud. It was about 12.30 in the morning.*

Susan's experience made perfect sense in human terms. She was alone and frightened and an angel came to protect her. After the experience, she felt calm and the birth was easy from then on.

The majority of angelic encounters do happen not to the spiritually elevated but to ordinary men, women and children at times when they are alone and vulnerable and call out for help or support. None of the above four accounts was dramatic, but all were immensely reassuring, precious and significant, demonstrating that there is more to life than the material world.

2

How to Tell Angels Are Around You

Many of us are touched by angelic energies without realising it, because angels tend to wait until we are ready to welcome them into our lives before they make contact. Our hard-working guardian angel is always there, moving hazards out of our way, nudging us back on track when we lose our direction, and picking up the pieces of a shattered ego or heart.

Other helper angels are also ready to enter our lives at particular times when we would benefit from their wisdom. But because the modern world, even for country dwellers, is often noisy and frantic, we may miss the signs of their presence. Being polite, angels tend not to intrude (except in an emergency) until we acknowledge one of the signals they have given.

Our ancestors, who had no planes, cars or high-speed trains, travelled long distances by horse and cart or on foot and would huddle round the fireside during the long winter evenings. But in a world of 24/7 heating, lighting, mobile phones and countless satellite channels, we may not experience much silence or stillness. My Swedish publisher and I have a long-standing joke every time I go to Sweden, that we will go for a walk in the beautiful forests that surround her home. But we are always busy working, and as I get back on the high-speed train to the airport, we say: 'Next time we will go for our walk.' For this reason, this chapter outlines some simple ways to encourage inner stillness. As a result, you will increase your ability to recognise the spiritual presence of angels.

Silence and stillness are states in which we can most easily become aware of an angelic presence – and later in the book I describe how you can make a special angel place for strengthening the connection (see page 30). However, angels are remarkably adaptable and will make their presence felt even in the busiest street or most high-tech office, if you are aware of the signs. We will be looking at how you can encourage some of these initial contacts throughout the book. The following are some of the many signs that angels have entered your life. If you are in the habit of working with angels, you will no doubt have your own to add to my list:

○ Tiny white feathers appearing in unexpected places or at unexpected times

○ A shimmering sensation seen out of the corner of your eye when you are trying to make a decision or resolve a dilemma

- The tinkling of tiny bells, especially in the early morning or late evening when everything else is silent

- A butterfly or beautiful moth flying in through the door or window out of season and settling close to you. (Be sure to let it out)

- A small blue or white bird perching outside your window and appearing unafraid when you move near. It will appear when you feel sad or anxious

- A series of light beams or rainbows dancing in a room on a dark day or when there is no obvious light source

- A sense of complete peace flooding through you at a time when you were panicking or feeling stressed

- A sense of anticipation and excitement – like on Christmas morning – when you wake on a perfectly ordinary day

- Soft laughter in your ear when you are feeling unhappy or lonely

- Full-blown choral music, perhaps just for a minute or two, that no-one else seems aware of

- A sudden, wonderful fragrance that smells like a mixture of your favourite flowers but is more beautiful and intense

- A feeling of being enclosed, just for a second, in a soft, feathery blanket (called an angelic hug), usually when you feel alone or unloved

- A piece of paper blowing out of your hand when a breeze springs up out of nowhere. As you chase, the paper seems to pause for you to catch up before blowing on, at last coming to a rest so you can pick it up. The breeze disappears as suddenly as it came. Young playful angels love doing this to get your attention

- Someone calling your name two or three times in a rich, melodious tone that makes you feel both happy and sad at once

- Sudden unexpected help that has vanished by the time you turn to thank the Good Samaritan: the man who carries your heavy case across a station bridge when you have only two minutes to catch a connecting train; the woman who waits with you till a taxi cab unexpectedly materialises in a remote place (usually the very human driver is puzzled why he was there at all)

- Your baby or small child looking straight ahead and gurgling or waving at the ceiling towards what seems to be a dancing light or rainbow that moves in unison with them as they move. Children are always surrounded by angels, usually the chubby kind you see in old paintings (artists may have recalled them from their own childhood)

○ Your pet cat or dog rolling over and making contented sounds as though being stroked (angels love animals)

○ A sudden radiance around your outline, especially your head, when you look into a mirror or a pool of water, even on a dark day

○ Seeing an unmistakeable figure of light in the first seconds after you wake, which disappears when you blink

○ Seeing angels in the clouds or at a sunset over a hill and discovering that the place is called the Hill of Angels because there have been so many angelic sightings there. Angels are drawn to places of natural beauty

○ Being suddenly pulled back from crossing a road or finding your car doesn't respond when you try to pull out into the fast lane, only to realise seconds later that a vehicle you hadn't seen was hurtling towards you

○ The sense of a benevolent presence walking beside you on a lonely path or road when you feel nervous

○ What seems like silver glitter falling on you from above, but when you look up, there is no obvious source

○ Seeing an angel guiding the smaller angels at a Christmas nativity play, then looking again to find no-one is there

○ Walking effortlessly up a steep hill laden with bags or finding that the journey home on a day when you are tired is noticeably shorter

○ A favourite hymn or prayer from childhood suddenly flowing through your mind at a point of crisis, then the crisis disappearing

○ Rainbow lights appearing in a room

○ A sudden sensation of warmth as though someone had switched on a fan heater

○ The sensation that someone is gently touching your shoulders

○ A book falling off a shelf open at a page that has the answer or information you were seeking

○ Your eyes filling with tears of happiness for no apparent reason

Angelic communication often begins as a slowly growing awareness that you are loved and blessed. The signs increase until at last you stop rushing around and tune in. If you experience any of the manifestations above – or have similar experiences that you recognise as the presence of angels – don't forget to say thank you softly.

3

Beginning Angel Communication

In this chapter we will be exploring a basic technique for talking with your guardian angel and looking at at different ways of changing this ritual by using light, colour, crystals and so on. As you become increasingly familiar with your guardian angel and with the methods that work for you, you will find you need to use fewer techniques and will be aware of your guardian angel whenever you call on him or her. We will also be looking at keeping an angel diary.

Guardian angels

Most important and closest to us of all the angels is our guardian angel, the special angel that closes the channel (situated at the fontanel) to the spiritual realms after the spirit enters our body at birth. Before that moment, the spirit can wander quite freely between the mother's womb and the heavens. It is said by some people that the other angels cry when the infant's spirit begins its earthly journey.

Your guardian angel never leaves you and at the end of your life will help your spirit rise and return to the golden place from which it came. A number of people have reported seeing a golden light leaving the body of a dead person. Frequently people who are dying have also spoken of an angelic presence near them during their last days or hours.

During childhood we may still see our guardian angel; however, children often prefer to play with little spirit-guide friends, referred to by adults as imaginary friends. As the child becomes more immersed in the physical and mental world, so the guardian angel is less involved in day-to-day events.

Let me tell you about Myrtle's childhood angel friends. I met Myrtle when I attended a Quaker Church with my children some years ago. She was in her eighties then, and very wise and an inspiration to everyone. She told me this story from her early life:

> When I was a child in southern India, several little angel friends used to come and play with me. In the afternoons I would be put for a rest on the veranda and the angels used to stand on the balustrade and come down to play if I called to them. Sometimes they stood around

my mattress and told me tales of how they helped people who were in trouble, guided them over difficult mountain passes and through hazardous places and protected them from danger. I never told anyone my secret. It was too precious.

When I was 13 I was sent to England to boarding school. I was so far from home and I was very miserable. But my angel friends helped me and stayed with me until I settled down. I still think about my angel friends, as they were such an important part of my early life, and sometimes now I feel their presence.

I recently learned that Myrtle died soon after she recounted this experience.

When we reach adulthood, our guardian angel tends to take a back seat and our spirit guides become more important, as they are more attuned to daily life and its problems. Our guardian angel may watch from a little distance, hoping that as well as following our all-important earthly path we may still remember that we are spiritual beings in an earthly body.

Encounters with a guardian angel

The following stories are two examples of how a person first encountered their guardian angel. Courtney, an art student who now lives in Washington State, USA, was 18 when his angel came to his rescue.

Courtney was driving in Oregon when he fell asleep at the wheel of his car late one night. It crashed into a concrete bridge and turned over. He was woken by the impact, upside-down, covered in glass, in darkness, on a deserted country road. Suddenly an urgent voice told him to get out of the car, but he could not find the seat-belt release. He panicked, but then felt a hand gently guiding him to find and unfasten the release button. As he tried to crawl across the crushed roof of the car, he cried out for help, then suddenly found himself floating outside the car, surrounded by a light more brilliant than any he had ever seen. He closed his eyes because the light was so dazzling. When he opened them, the radiance was gone. But the danger was not over. As he stood alone in the darkness, stunned, a voice told him to run as fast as he could. Seconds later, the car burst into flames and was completely destroyed.

So fierce had been the impact of the crash that the engine had gone through the floor. Courtney, however, escaped with minor cuts and bruises and was able to walk along the road to find help. Most amazing of all, the only spot on the car's roof that was not completely crushed was the small area in which Courtney's head had impacted.

Layla, an astrologer who lives in the north-west of England, is in her twenties. She was sceptical about the idea of guardian angels and, unlike Courtney, was not in a crisis situation when she met hers. She told me:

I've been doing readings at a local holistic shop recently. The owner of the shop, Malcolm, has told me that he is very interested in angels and that he often finds feathers in his shop that he takes to be communication from his angels. I was teasing him about this yesterday. 'More like moulting pigeons,' I laughed.

Later on that day, as I was sitting relaxing with a cup of coffee, a tiny white feather floated down and landed on the table. I showed Malcolm the feather, and he said it must be my angel trying to get in touch.

This morning I was doing an internet reading for a lady in the USA. One of her questions was: 'Do I have a guardian angel and what is his name?'

As soon as I read her question I felt I should close my eyes. When I did this I saw in my mind a piece of white paper with a word in neat black letters. The word was 'Hadiel'. This looked like a nonsense word to me, but I typed it into my web browser and found it in a list of angel names. Hadiel is a very obscure angel and all I could find out was that he governs the sign of Libra.

All the way through this lady's reading I had been telling her she needed to bring more balance and harmony into her life, the qualities of Libra. Her star sign was also Libra. So I sat there for a moment letting it all sink in. I thought to myself: 'If that's what her angel is called, what's the name of my angel?'

I closed my eyes and saw the name Chaldiel. I found this angel's name in a long list on the internet; he is the angel of astrology and prophecy. I won't be teasing Malcolm about his angel feathers in the future.

Layla's encounter may not be as dramatic as Courtney's, but it should not be undervalued, because these three small incidents led her to an awareness of her special angel.

For most of us, the connection with our angel is quite subtle and won't stand up to the scrutiny of formal tests or make a television documentary. But what matters is that the angelic communication is of meaning and value to us individually and enriches our lives in some way.

Occasionally, you may come across people who tell you they deal only with the top Archangels, who have entrusted them with the secrets of humanity – the ultimate ego trip! In fact, we can all draw Archangel energies into our life and channel Archangel wisdom – and this book will show you ways to do this; however, it is with our guardian angel that we will have the most frequent and closest links. He is our best celestial friend.

So value your own path and take each small sign of connection as a blessing and confirmation that you are on the right track.

Contacting your guardian angel

If you already communicate with your guardian angel, you can use the ideas in this section to enrich your connection and perhaps identify other angels who are around you. You will notice that some of the methods I suggest mirror the spontaneous ways angels try to attract our attention. All such rituals are highly personal, so please feel free to combine elements of two or more methods. If it feels right to you, then it is right.

What follows is a simple connection ritual. We will then gradually build on the information you gain from it so you can incorporate other elements into the sequence.

Preparation

○ You can work indoors or outdoors, but you should find a place that feels comfortable and where you can completely relax and be totally without distraction. If you want to work outdoors, find a secluded beautiful spot where you feel quite safe.

○ If you are working indoors, do it in the evening or early morning. If you are working are outdoors, choose a time when there is sun-, moon- or starlight – all of which are excellent for angel work.

○ Ensure that you have at least half an hour and will not be disturbed.

○ Switch off all phones.

○ Wear something loose and comfortable.

○ Before you begin, have a bath by candlelight or soft natural light, using lavender or rose foam or oils.

○ If you are working in the open air, pour a little natural mineral water in a dish and splash it on your hairline, your brow, your throat and your pulse points to cleanse your aura, or energy field.

Relaxation

○ Sit or lie on a rug, cushions or a bed and breathe regularly and gently, listening to your breath but not worrying about counting breaths or establishing a pattern. You know how to breathe, so just enjoy the process rather than trying to control it.

○ Allow yourself to relax completely. Don't force anything. Picture soft fluffy banks of clouds or thick warm snowflakes falling, and gently push away any intrusive thoughts.

Become aware of your angel

○ After a minute or so, you may sense or see your angel in your mind through clairvoyant, or psychic, vision. The angel may be surrounded by coloured mists or perhaps in a beautiful garden with flowers you can smell.

○ Alternatively – or in addition – you may hear a deep melodious voice in your ear or just sense the presence and perhaps feel a light touch.

○ If you don't see or hear anything, don't worry – just sensing the angel's presence is every bit as good. In time, the clairvoyant (psychic vision) and clairaudient (psychic hearing) channels will open.

Speak with your angel

○ There are no right or wrong methods to communicate with your angel. However, a good way to begin when you feel connected is to speak softly as though to a dear friend you have not seen for many years. You don't need to use formal language, but you may find that a childhood prayer or favourite hymn flows through your mind.

Establish a lasting link with your angel

○ When the encounter seems to be fading, touch your heart with your power hand (the one you write with). You may see or sense your angel doing the same thing, like a mirror image; if not, imagine the angel doing this. Say:

I reach out with my heart.

This links your heart chakra (a chakra is a psychic energy centre) with the angelic heart.

○ Now touch your throat with the same hand. Again, you may see or sense your angel doing the same thing; if not, imagine the angel doing this. Say:

I reach out with my words.

This links your throat chakra with the angelic voice.

○ Touch the centre of your brow with the same hand. Again, you may see or sense your angel doing the same thing; if not, imagine the angel doing this. Say:

I reach out with my mind and with my spirit.

This links your brow chakra (or third – psychic – eye), with the angelic spirit.

○ Finally, touch the centre of your hairline with the same hand. Again, you may see or sense your angel doing the same thing; if not, imagine the angel doing this. Say:

I reach out with my soul to the place from where I came.

This links your crown chakra with the evolved soul of your angel.

For future angelic contact, you can begin by making these four movements and speaking the words – or ones that seem right for you. By the fourth movement you should see or sense your angel responding. You can end connection in the same way.

If, after some weeks or months of practice, you want to see your angel externally, perform the ritual in front of a mirror lit by candlelight, sunlight or moonlight, or a light-filled pool outdoors (during a full moon is ideal). If you close your eyes slowly and open them equally slowly, you may momentarily see your angel in the reflective surface next to your own reflection. If not, it is not the right time, so be patient and enjoy the wonder of your present level of contact. One day you will see your angel, when you least expect him or her.

Using fragrance in angelic contact

The presence of angels is often heralded by an accompanying fragrance that is not quite earthly. This angelic perfume is similar to rose or lotus but has a particularly wonderful purity. The fragrances that accompany angels or angelic energies have been described as predominantly floral, identified variously by different people as: apple blossom, carnation, geranium, hibiscus, honeysuckle, hyacinth, jasmine, lavender, lilac, lilies, linden blossom, lotus, mimosa, neroli (orange blossom), rose and violet.

You can begin your angelic work by burning one of the angelic fragrances listed above as a scented candle or fragrance oil. Alternatively, inhale a good-quality perfume or scented water, or the natural flowers or blossoms.
If you are using a scented candle, you can gaze into the flame, allowing your eyes to relax, and perhaps see your angel around the candle flame.

In time you will know your guardian angel's special scent. You can then use it, instead of the more general scents suggested above, as a sign that you seek to contact him or her.

Using light in angelic contact

To begin with, moving lights are best, so if you are using a candle, ensure that a window is slightly open or a small fan is switched on so that the flame slowly dances. (Take care to place your candle where soft furnishings and other flammable objects cannot be blown into the flame.) If you are working outdoors, a place where sunlight or moonlight ripples through water or is filtered through leaves is ideal. Other possibilities are:

○ Drape small, twinkling fairy lights – the kind that flash on and off – in a darkened room or garden.

○ Use a fibre optic lamp with silver and gold beams. It is sometimes possible to find beautiful fibre optic flowers or small trees. These are ideal for angel work.

○ In daylight, rainbows and dancing circles of light can be created by hanging clear crystals or crystal pendulums at windows to catch the natural light. Experiment with different angles and heights.

○ Perspex rainbows on a window likewise reflect rainbow rays on a sunny day.

○ An indoor or outdoor water feature or outdoor fountain will form rainbows and light-filled water droplets, as well as adding the dimension of sound.

Using crystals in angelic contact

Crystals are a natural medium through which to merge with angel energies. Clear quartz crystal spheres, especially those with inclusions or flaws, are probably the best of all. Even a tiny crystal sphere will act as a channel, and if you hold your ball to any light source you may see a tiny sparkling image of your special angel quite clearly inside. You may also hear the angelic voice in your ear. If this doesn't happen straight away, relax, and in time it will.

Other small crystals also amplify angel presences. Hold the individual crystals in your power hand and close your eyes to focus the energies. The following crystals are especially good for angel work.

Amethyst: especially the soft, translucent, deep purple kind.

Angelite: pale or mid- to celestial blue, with white veins like angel wings.

Aqua aura: an electric sky blue, transparent crystal quartz made by bombarding clear quartz with molten gold. You can gaze within this crystal to see your angel or hold it and close your eyes as described above.

Celestite or celestine: pale to mid-blue, semi-transparent, these look like ice crystals. Celestite comes from the Latin word for the heavens. It is called 'the stone of heaven', and is said to be created by the song of the celestial angel choirs. It is especially good for use with sacred music.

Cobalt or titanium aura: made when molecules of pure cobalt are bonded by the natural electric charge of clear quartz, cobalt aura is brilliant shades of royal blue, violet and gold. Titanium aura is darker with more purple. I have found these particularly effective as angel crystals during recent workshops.

Fluorites: the dual-colour green and lavender or deeper purple are very subtle crystals and are useful if you find angel communication difficult because you have a very logical mind.

Opal aura: a wonderful, gleaming, opalescent rainbow crystal, said to link you with your personal guardian angel. Hold it to candlelight or hold the rainbow in your power hand.

Phantom quartz: clear quartz containing a shadow or ghost crystal within, formed when a crystal stops growing, often from a chlorite crystal with quartz enclosing it. This crystal offers a natural doorway to other dimensions.

Rose quartz: gentle pink, transparent or translucent crystal, ideal for children to feel the protection of their guardian angel at night.

Rutilated quartz: contains golden rutiles – called angel hair – which are said to help us to hear angel song.

Using sound in angelic contact

Many people have heard angelic music. In the Alister Hardy Research Centre I came across the story of two teenage Irish girls who independently reported hearing heavenly choirs singing at the time their elderly aunt was dying. Both girls were in different locations at the time. In Chapter 5, I describe how Jacky was helped to soothe her sick child by angelic music (see page 51).

Any sacred music evokes the presence of angels, but church choirs, Gregorian chants and, of course, Christmas carols are especially effective. Angels love to hear children singing, so when your child is happily walking up and down humming, you can be sure angels are near. As well as the traditional harps, Tibetan singing bowls and panpipes are very evocative, as are dolphin or wolf calls set to music.

Play the music very softly as a background to your angelic encounter and let the sounds carry you until you can perhaps hear slower, sweeter angelic singing in the background or a softer musical resonance, sometimes called the music of the spheres or planets.

What is your angel's name?

When you have connected with your angel, you may want to ask his or her name.

We know from traditional writings that there are millions of angels – so many that they could not be counted; therefore it is not surprising that relatively few angel names are officially recorded. Little is known about the identity of all but the main Archangels and those angels associated with the seasons and the zodiac. What information we do have has been built up over the years, most of it collected during the Middle Ages. It is from this traditional medieval angelology that most of the information in this book derives.

But it may be that angel names are purely human concepts and that angels use names because we need them to or ask them to. So if the name you are given by your angel isn't recognisable even after searching the internet and angel books, just accept it. Our knowledge is far from complete. Focus on the wondrous blessing of having a relationship with your special guardian rather than worrying about verification in the world's terms.

It is a human characteristic to categorise and list everything, and a human failing that if we can't verify something – whether it is an extra-terrestrial being, a psychic experience or an angelic presence – we arrogantly say it can't possibly exist. I believe that if we can suspend our logical analytical minds we can more easily connect with spiritual experience.

Remember, then, that even the well-documented angelic hierarchies described at the end of this chapter are human assignations and categories, so if they do not feel right for you, don't use them.

Using alphabet cards to write your angel's name

Before seeking to identify an angel, be it your own or that of someone you are working with, always ask first if you may know their name. Layla's method of identifying angels by picturing the names written in black on white is very effective (see page 23). The following simple system, which anyone can use, is my favourite:

O Write each letter of the alphabet on a different card.

O Place the cards in a circle, face down, in any order.

O Moving clockwise around the circle, hold a pendulum over each letter in turn. Ask your angel to spell out their name by causing the pendulum to vibrate or pull down as though weighed down by a heavy hand over each relevant letter. You will feel the unmistakable pull over the right letters. The angel doesn't take over your body but merely guides your hand.

O See if the chosen letters make a name in the order you picked them. If not, keep rearranging them until you have a name. Be aware that while angels communicate in the language we most naturally speak and understand, traditional angelic names can be very strange, with Zs, Xs and Ys in odd places if it is a Middle Eastern name, or vowels apparently missing.

O If you still can't find anything resembling a name by rearranging the letters and checking on an internet search engine, then write the name in incense-stick smoke in the air, choosing the letter order that most nearly makes a name. Because the communication is across dimensions, it may be that you have not picked a relevant letter because the pendulum hesitated over one and you moved on. As you write the letters, the full name will come into your mind.

Using automatic handwriting to write your angel's name

Another method of discovering your angel's name is by automatic handwriting. Use a green ink pen, the kind with a nib if you can find one, and cream or white paper of as good a quality as you can obtain. Old-fashioned writing sets with paper and envelopes are ideal for angelic communication.

Ask your angel aloud for the name by which you may call him or her. Traditional angelologists, of course, regarded angels as male, but in modern times, female energies have come more to the fore. In fact, because they are not human, angels are probably androgynous. Because this is hard for many of us to relate to, your personal angel may appear as either male or female, according to which you are most comfortable with.

You can also use this method to ask questions of your guardian angel and also other helper angels (whom I describe in Chapter 5).

○ Prepare yourself as usual to contact your angel and have your pen and paper ready in front of you.

○ Hold the pen in a relaxed way in the hand you normally write with and allow the words to flow through your pen and onto the paper without trying to rationalise or analyse.

○ When you sense there is no more, thank the angel and sit and read what you have written. You may get a single name or a whole lot of information about your angel after the name.

○ Once you have the name, you can ask questions, if you wish, allowing your pen to write the answers dictated by your angel. Again, you are not being taken over, but your angel is guiding your hand.

Making a special angel place

You have already chosen a tranquil place (or places) in which you make contact with your angel. You might like to take this a stage further by creating a special angel place where you can talk to angels, carry out angel rituals and sit to absorb the peace when you feel anxious or sad.

Some people adopt a spare room that is currently used for accumulating clutter best dispersed; others adapt a garden shed. But you don't need a whole room. If all you can spare is a small, flat surface – such as a table or unit in your bedroom – you can still make it a sacred space. It is not selfish to want to make a centre of sanctity within your home. After even a few weeks of having a sacred area in your home, you will notice that the whole atmosphere has lifted. Family and visitors will become more peaceful and centred as the angelic energies pervade the entire dwelling.

Ensure that the area is warm and well ventilated. Have comfortable seating for carrying out rituals. If you can, you might like to include a bed or couch to lie and relax on when you are carrying out angel meditation or receiving healing from an angel. Big cushions are ideal. To enclose the area and separate it from the everyday world, you could hang floaty drapes – which can be bought very cheaply from ethnic craft stores and on-line.

The area should include a flat surface, on which you place the following:

○ A silver or white cloth.

○ Four small crystal angels, to represent the four directions. Small free-standing crystal angels intended for pendants can be bought quite cheaply, and they are available in different crystals. Traditional colours are green or brown for the north; yellow or grey for the east; red, orange or clear for the south; and blue or silvery (like moonstone) for the west. If you prefer, you can use a clear crystal angel for each direction.

○ In the centre of your four angels, set a flat dish or plate of any kind you like. This is to hold crystals or other items – such as a favourite pendant or ring – that you wish the angels to empower. You can also set your angel letters (see page 75) on the dish during rituals. Glass is often used on angel altars for holding items.

○ In the north, to the left of your angel, place small dish of fragrant dried petals or pot pourri. You can dry your own petals from favourite bouquets or bunches of flowers and keep them in a sealed, dark glass jar. This represents the Earth element and the Earth angels.

○ In the east of the altar, place a ceramic incense-stick holder and a supply of floral incense sticks in a jar. For appropriate fragrances, see page 26. These represent the Air element and the Air angels.

○ In the south, place a candle, if possible made of beeswax, because bees are messengers associated with the Virgin Mary and her mother St Anne, who are often regarded as the mother and grandmother of the angels. Scented candles in soft shades can also be used here. This represents the Fire element and the Fire angels.

○ In the west, place a small glass or dish of sparkling mineral water. If you wish, add a drop or two of your favourite fragrance. This represents the Water element and the Water angels.

○ You might also like to add small glass candlesticks (available quite cheaply) and other glass items to your altar.

Now you have created a perfect place for communicating with your angels.

Keeping an angel journal

You may wish to start an angel journal as a special record of your angel pathway and as a heritage for your children and your children's children. You can write down any messages received and any images or impressions about angels and their realms that you encounter as you continue your angelic contact and find out more about angels through reading and research.

Use a book with plain white or cream sheets and keep a special pen for your journal; green ink is good, because green is considered to have special properties relating to spirit communication. You might like to use this pen for all your angel communications.

Sit quietly in soft sunlight or candlelight and copy out the most important parts of any communications with your angels. Although you can channel angel messages directly into your journal, some people prefer to channel onto paper and then copy the message into their journal later, adding any insights they have in relation to it.

You can list any angels you encounter and include any background information you discover about them via the internet or books. You can also include postcards of angel images. Art galleries are a good source. They usually have a good selection of angel paintings.

Keep notes of any healing sent to others or requested for yourself through your healing angel, whom you will meet later in the book (see page 53), and any angel lore or stories you encounter that seem relevant to you. Note also any crystals or fragrances that work well for you and angelic prayers or chants you have found or created.

There is no limit to what you can put in your journal, and it will make inspiring reading when you feel tired or dispirited. One day, your journal may become the basis for your own angel book. Whether or not you choose to publish it, it will be a legacy for future generations.

4

The Angelic Hierarchy

In this chapter, we will be looking in more detail at the hierarchy of angels and how the different levels relate to each other. The angelic hierarchy consists of the nine traditional orders of angels that were recorded from the visions of the fifth-century churchman Dionysus. The angels are divided into three choirs, or spheres, and each contains three smaller choirs, or ranks, of angels.

Below is a list of the ranks, starting with those furthest away from humanity and closest to divinity, and ending with our own guardian angels, which are the lowest order and live closest to us. In descending order they are:

First choir
○ Seraphim

○ Cherubim/Kerubim

○ Thrones

Second choir
○ Dominions

○ Virtues

○ Powers

Third choir
○ Principalities

○ Archangels

○ Angels (including guardian angels)

This hierarchy can provide a useful framework and make the higher realms of angels seem more accessible as you continue to develop your communication with angels. Bear in mind, however, that Dionysus was writing 1,500 years ago, in an age and culture very different from ours. Some people find the whole concept of ranks of angels old-fashioned. If the choirs of angels aren't helpful to you, then simply continue to work with angels on an individual level. Bear in mind, too, that although Dionysus describes specific characteristics of the different classes of angel, no-one really has a precise knowledge of the angelic realms, and you may find that these descriptions do not resonate with you. If that is the case, trust yourself.

Whenever you are working with angels, burn the appropriate colour of candle and the incense listed, or burn a fragrance oil of the kind listed for each individual angelic group. You could also hold a favourite angel statue or one of the tiny altar angels and allow images and ideas to come. Remember to keep records of your experiences in your journal.

It is important always to remember that even the most powerful angels are not allowed to override free will in humans. This is why their work is so difficult and bad things do still happen in the world.

The first choir

The three categories of angels within this highest sphere work on a universal level and are concerned with how divinity is expressed through creation. They touch us through the divine spark within us all, whether you think of divinity as God, the Goddess or a universal power of light and goodness. They operate on the level of thought and are called the Seraphim, the Cherubim and the Thrones.

The Seraphim

The Seraphim have been described as concerned with the harmony or vibrations of the universe, and they regulate its movements.

They have six wings and four faces, so they can see in all directions, and they carry flaming swords. They have been called the angels of pure love, light and fire. They ensure that divine love is transmitted through the different levels so that eventually it reaches humans, animals and plants.

The Seraphim's light is so brilliant that only the highest spiritual forms in the heavens and the supreme Archangel Michael can look on them, and they stand guard over the veil that separates pure divinity from creation. They sing the praises of God and can occasionally be heard by mortals – they were heard by the shepherds at the very first Christmas. It is from the Seraphim that we get the 'Holy, holy, holy' chants in many prayers and hymns, this being the way their hymns of praise are said to begin.

○ The Seraphim are led by Archangel Uriel, the angel of transformation.

○ Call upon them if you are working for planetary healing, world peace or humanitarian causes and whenever you sing or chant.

○ Burn a bright red candle and frankincense incense.

The Cherubim

The Cherubim (or Kerubim) are below the Seraphim in the hierarchy. They have been portrayed as the guardians of the fixed stars, the constellations and all the galaxies, and as the warrior angels. They keep the heavenly records of the lives of humans and are the angels who transmit light and knowledge through the universe to humans. They protect temples and great cathedrals and churches, as well as sacred sites in all ages and cultures.

They have been described as dazzlingly radiant blue angels, sometimes with four faces and wings, also as winged sphinxes or lions with four beautiful faces, many all-seeing eyes and wings. They are linked to the four winds.

O The Cherubim are led by the Archangel Jophiel.

O Call upon them for protection, especially of those who are made vulnerable because of war, who are in spiritual darkness or who suffer material poverty, and for increased wisdom and knowledge.

O Burn a blue candle and sandalwood incense.

The Thrones

These angels are the bringers of justice and oversee the planets (which also have individual Archangels). Thrones are concerned with cruelty and suppression, and send healing energies to persecuted nations and groups who are unable to live, learn, work or worship freely.

They are called the charioteers, or sometimes the chariots of divinity, and have been described as brilliant spinning wheels of light with many eyes. They are responsible for spreading goodness and justice though the world.

O The Thrones are led by the Archangel Japhkiel.

O Call upon them to assist in any matter of injustice, whether regarding an oppressed minority or an endangered species being wiped out by human greed or indifference, or when there is a series of global disasters caused by ozone damage or the cutting down of rainforests.

O Burn an indigo candle and pine or cinnamon incense.

The second choir

As we move closer to humanity, the roles of the different orders of angels become more specific. The second-sphere angels form a connection between the highest realms and the lower ones, and these angels interact more directly with us.

The Dominions

Dominions are said to be the oldest of the angels (in the sense that they were the first to be created) and are the leader angels, carrying orbs and sceptres. They have been called priests or princes and function as the control centre for the other ranks of angels, higher and lower. Dominions ensure that things happen. They are also concerned with how spiritual principles operate through earthly authority. In this they have a hard job, because people – especially world leaders – won't always listen.

The Dominions perform major miracles and are said to have saved earth from potential collisions with asteroids, as well as performing the earthly miracles, such as the parting of the Red Sea, that are necessary to change the course of history when we go too badly wrong. Dominions can occasionally unleash less positive powers, such as the global flood that is described in many cultures – in stories of the sinking of Atlantis and the building of Noah's Ark – to sweep away what is no longer of good.

○ The Dominions are ruled by the Archangel Zadkiel.

○ Not the most comfortable angels to work with since they demand very high standards, the Dominions are nevertheless good for leadership issues at all levels and for giving courage, especially against seemingly impossible odds.

○ Burn an orange candle and sage incense.

The Virtues

The Virtues are gentler angels, associated with love and miracles on earth. They bring patience and quiet strength, and foster practical efforts for world peace through the work of organisations and individuals.

They are responsible for the natural world, ruling the weather and the elemental energies of Earth, Air, Fire and Water. They regulate rain and sunshine for growth and so bring material blessings and abundance. The Virtues also carry out the instructions of the Dominions.

We don't know much about the Virtues' appearance, except that they are often surrounded by mists or the colours of sunset and have starry crowns.

○ The Virtues are ruled by the Archangel Anael (also Hanael or Haniel).

○ Call upon them if you are trying hard to achieve something of worth in any area of your life, as these angels assist those who strive and don't give up. They are good for any rituals to protect your homeland and to bring peace between the peoples of different lands through sharing cultural knowledge. They are also helpful for tolerance of those who have different lifestyles, especially if they share our homeland.

○ Burn a pink or green candle and rose incense.

The Powers

The Powers are the cosmic police force. They not only deter wrongdoing, often with a timely warning, but also assist souls who are lost, either in life or after death, by sending angelic help. Powers have more and more work to do as humans invent ever more powerful weapons of destruction and as terrorism affects even peaceful lands.

Powers are the angels of birth and death, who ensure our guardians are with us as we enter and leave the world. As such they are often depicted in green, gold or red robes. These are the hosts of angels depicted in brilliant jewel-coloured robes in medieval paintings. They also help those with severe illness or disabilities to reach their potential and support those who care for them.

The Powers are also depicted as warrior angels, resplendent in gold and red armour and bearing shining swords. They organise the world's religions and try to stop people using religion as an excuse for war or intolerance, though – like all angels – they have to allow us ultimate free choice. If we listen, they will alert us through our intuitive senses and offer us protection.

○ The Powers are ruled by the Archangel Raphael.

○ Call upon them to protect your home and family, and also your neighbourhood and city.

○ Burn a yellow candle and rosemary or thyme incense.

The third choir

The third choir, which is closest to us, is the most accessible to us in our angel work. They are the Principalities, the Archangels, and the Angels, and they bring the higher work of the other spheres into a more specific human context.

The Principalities

The Principalities are concerned with the organisation of large groups of people in practical settings created for living or working in. They especially oversee the fair distribution of resources (another uphill task), discrimination issues and all teaching and learning situations, such as those in colleges, schools and universities. They also preside over alternative spirituality. They are called the ministering angels, a term sometimes applied to the Archangels and guardian angels as well.

Principalities look like ordinary angels but tend to be taller and more brilliant and have shimmering wings and haloes – again, you will see them depicted in medieval paintings. They are also concerned with the protection of wildlife – on a more practical level than the Thrones.

○ The Principalities are ruled by the Archangel Camael.

○ Call upon them for help with learning, with your spiritual path and with protecting your workplace, public buildings and artefacts, especially those concerned with knowledge and the local ecosystem.

○ Burn a silver candle and lavender incense.

The Archangels

The Archangels are the most fascinating of all the angels and operate on several levels of the hierarchy. Individual Archangels, such as Michael, work with the highest levels of angels and often have elevated roles within the seven heavens, which I discuss in more detail on pages 39–42. The Archangels also rule individual planets, seasons, directions, days of the week and hours of the day. They tend to be identifiable by individual names, robes and symbols. We will meet many of these individual Archangels in the following chapters.

Archangels have been seen as the supreme messengers in a number of religions down the ages. The four best-known Archangels are Raphael, Michael, Uriel and Gabriel who, through the centuries, have been assigned magical as well as religious significance. Two Archangels, Michael, Archangel of the sun, and Gabriel, Archangel of the moon, are mentioned frequently in the Old and New Testament Books of the Bible and the Koran. Raphael also appears in the Bible.

Archangels are concerned with our spiritual welfare and stand at the point where our personal concerns are joined to a sense of responsibility for the well-being of others and our planet.

O   The Archangels are ruled by Michael.

O   Work with Archangels when you have major issues in your life or you wish to work for global concerns such as world peace or the well-being of the environment.

O   Burn a gold candle and lotus or carnation incense.

For more information on the Archangels see Chapter 6.

The angels

This group includes our very own guardian angels, as well as angels of healing and nature, who live close to humans and can be easily contacted. They protect us and guide us throughout our lives.

Both you and your house will have a personal guardian angel, and I describe this angelic being and give you a lot more information in the following chapters. Each of us sees these personal angels in our own way.

O   The angels are ruled by Gabriel.

O   Call upon the angels for any private or family issue.

O   Burn a white candle and any floral incense.

How you work with angels is, as I have said, very much a personal thing. I find that it is easiest begin with realms closest to us, as they are most attuned to our everyday needs and therefore easier to contact. I suggest therefore that you start with the lower orders and gradually work up the angelic hierarchy over a period of months.

Where do angels live?

The answer to this question is everywhere, because physical matter does not bind them. However, since we human beings are more limited by our earthly thought processes, for thousands of years we have tried to describe the heavens where the angels dwell as we have seen them in dreams and visions. Thus there is more than one school of thought about what the angelic realms really are, each conceived by a different philosopher to try to convey the intensity of the other-worldly dimension they experienced.

Here I am going to take the system of seven ascending heavens that is recognised in Judaism, Christianity and Islam (although there is much debate over the proper order of the heavens). In some other systems there are ten heavens. Since what is generally considered as the Bible contains relatively little information about angels and the heavens, much of the wisdom we draw on comes from alternative mystical writings and religious books, for example the Hebrew Testament of the Twelve Patriarchs.

So consider the following as a stimulus for your imagination and a context to set angels into, like a glorious painting. In your mind you can colour the backdrop as richly as you wish, as the medieval painters did. This formal categorisation reminds us that angels are glorious and splendid, even those who act as our friends and guides.

If you feel inspired by the idea of the seven heavens, you might like to write or paint your impressions (abstract swirls of colour are fine). You could also create guided journeys through the seven heavens for yourself and friends and record them on to tape or CD.

Shamayim: the first (or lowest) heaven

Shamayim adjoins the Earth and is ruled by the Archangel Gabriel. It is the source of the clouds, the winds and the Higher Waters that send the rains. Here live 200 astronomer angels who rule over the stars. Here, too, are Adam and Eve, the first humans, now in a perfected form, showing that all of us can put right mistakes and go on to great things.

Visualise the first heaven as a starry plain with beautiful clouds, rainbows, soft blue crystal towers and deep blue, glass-domed observatories.

Raquia: the second heaven

Raquia is governed by the Archangel Zachariel (or Yahriel), whose name means 'remembrance of God', and the healer Archangel Raphael. It is the home of Jesus and his cousin John the Baptist and, according to Moses, the dwelling of the gigantic angel Nuriel, who is surrounded by 50 hosts of angels made from water and fire. This makes the Second Heaven the source of the elements Earth, Air, Fire and Water in their purest form.

However, Raquia is a bit of a gloomy place in some descriptions. According to the Prophet Enoch, in part of this heaven fallen angels are imprisoned in complete darkness awaiting final judgment. The idea of fallen or wicked angels derives from the fourth century CE, when the Church leaders were trying to work out how, if God created everything and was totally good, sin and evil could exist at all. So they came up with the idea of fallen or rebellious angels. All angels, they said, had free will and so chose to be evil (still not 100 per cent convincing).

Visualise the second heaven in bright daylight or soft, midnight blue, velvety darkness, with rushing rivers and waterfalls, tall volcanic mountains, and vivid sunrises and sunsets.

Shehaqim: the third heaven

Shehaqim is the place where manna, or heavenly honey, the food of the angels and favoured mortals, is made by the celestial bees and stored. It is ruled by Anahel, described as a prince of angels and a guardian of the west, and is the dwelling place of those angels who ease the passing of the dying and welcome the deceased after death. In the south of this heaven is a wonderful garden paradise, like the Garden of Eden, where the souls of those who have tried to live good lives come after death.

Some of our gloomier ancestors believed that hell was not beneath the ground but in the north of this realm. In more modern concepts of the afterlife, it is believed that some may be imprisoned by their own dark thoughts or deeds until they can recognise the help around them that will lead them into the light and forgiveness.

Visualise the third heaven fragrant with thousands upon thousands of beautiful flowers, from which the celestial bees take pollen, and brightly coloured butterflies – it is like the most beautiful garden you can imagine.

Machanon: the fourth heaven

Machanon is ruled by Michael, the supreme Archangel, and is the location of the heavenly Jerusalem, the Holiest Temple and its Altar. The heavenly Jerusalem is the splendid jewelled city of light described in the New Testament Book of Revelations. Here, too, dwells Sandalaphon, the prayer gatherer. He is described as a towering Archangel of light, with a blazing halo and an olive branch of peace in his left hand. He helps to carry the prayers of humans to God and protects unborn children.

Visualise the fourth heaven as the most beautiful city you have ever seen, but far more splendid, with jewelled gateways and shimmering marble and glass walls, and wonderful grassy fields where tiny cherubs play.

Mathey: the fifth heaven

Mathey is ruled by the Archangel Sharquiel, who is brighter, taller and more glorious than any other of its enormous inhabitants – for in this heaven live magnificent gigantic angels with crowns on their heads, indicating that they are Lords among angels. They are sometimes called the Good Grigori or Good Watchers, and a shimmering throne said to be seven times brighter than the noonday sun in summer is also to be found in this land. Around this throne, ministering angels sing God's praises.

In less benign versions of Mathey, on the northern borders are the fallen Watchers, or fallen Grigori angels – another example of the way the early Church Fathers explained evil. The Watchers never sleep and it was said that when they were sent to earth, some fell in love with mortal women and now kneel silently in shame. Their half-human children may be an explanation of super-races such as the Atlanteans and of the Ancient Egyptian deities, both of whom brought advanced civilisations to relatively primitive peoples within a short period of history.

Visualise the fifth heaven as a realm of shimmering light, inhabited by huge angelic forms of light and filled with melodious choral song that may occasionally be heard on earth.

Zebul: the sixth heaven

Zebul (meaning 'temple') is the most mystical of the realms, described as a fusion of snow, ice and fire (recalling the Viking myth of the creation of the world through the union of fire and ice). It is a place where extremes and opposites meet to make a power greater than the original forces in their dynamic coming together. This heaven has dual rulers. Zebul, after whom the realm is named, presides during the day, Sabbath at night. Zebul is a high angel of pure white, while Sabbath, who orders the weekly sacred rest day (in Judaism Saturday, in Islam Friday, and in Christianity Sunday) and all holy ceremonies, sits on a throne of glory.

In the sixth heaven live seven golden phoenixes and seven mighty Cherubim with radiant blue rays, as well as many other wise angels who are not named. These angels of knowledge study astronomy and order the seasons, time, the turning of the natural world and the life cycle of humans.

Picture this land as ice and snow that never melts in spite of brilliant fiery sun, with misty bubbling hot springs and huge marble halls of learning.

Araboth: the seventh heaven

Araboth, the highest realm, is difficult even to imagine, let alone express in human terms. Here is found the veil that obscures the sight of God from all except those chosen to receive a glimpse, as the prophet Isaiah was said to have done in a vision that blinded him.

This heaven is ruled by Zagzagel, who speaks every language in the world, who gave Moses the Ten Commandments in the Burning Bush and who teaches all the other angels and Archangels their mission. Cassiel, the shadowy Archangel of Silence and Tears, who weeps for the sorrows of the world, also presides here, and here, too, dwell the Seraphim.

Visualise the seventh heaven as a place of brilliance but also dark shadows, the merging of gold and silver, darkness and light; it emits the radiance of the largest and most perfectly faceted diamond, and is a place where a second is the same as a hundred lifetimes. Here, if you are lucky, you may receive one glimpse of whatever is for you beauty and perfection.

5

Working with Guardian and Healing Angels

In this chapter we will be exploring ways to work with guardian angels, including the household guardian that every home has, and angels of healing.

Angels can help us in many ways, but sometimes we need to make a conscious effort to tune in to their energies when our daily lives demand that we spend so much time and energy on worldly matters. There are many small ways in which you can begin to make angelic contact even in the most pressurised existence. In this chapter I will be suggesting some of them.

Guardian angels

Some people believe that we have two guardian angels – one to our right, the other to our left – but for many of us our angel is like a more perfect version of ourselves that helps us to grow spiritually.

Because we live in a scientifically based world, we are often unwilling to accept the existence of guardian angels without proof. The danger of this approach is that we may miss spiritual experiences because they do not fit into our carefully ordered world-view.

Charlie is in his forties and lives in Sundsvall, Sweden. He was talking to his wife about guardian angels and said he would only believe in them if he were given proof. The next second, he felt someone touching his arm and was aware of someone very tall behind him. Then he was pushed down onto a table. He said he felt as though a fire was going through him. After that he never doubted the existence of angels again.

Pehr, today a well-known medium in Sweden, now knows that he has always been protected by angels. In his teenage years, however, he blocked out awareness of the angelic forces around him because of the pressures of his life and because he was often anxious and depressed. Only looking back on his experiences could Pehr say: 'My angel was with me all the time.' He was in his early twenties when he first truly encountered his guardian angel. He told me:

I first actually saw my personal angel when I was doing my Reiki initiation ceremony in 1992. I felt strange vibrations and saw an older female angel with a beautiful face and pure white wings. After that I have often seen women angels with white wings. My angel's eyes were so special, ice-blue and very clear, and she was smiling. It was a big feeling of being loved and held, and I cried and became a new person from that moment. It answered a lot of my earlier confusion.

My angel has enfolded me many times in moments of danger. I am convinced she was the one who protected me between the ages of 13 and 15. I did not want to go to school because the other boys would hurt me and would push my face in the snow. I was so depressed and blocked that I could not see my angel, but many times I escaped the bullying and felt her with me like a kind mother.

She also enfolded me in protection when I was 18 and riding my horse across the snow. There was a hole beside the road where the snow had been cleared away. The horse stumbled and I fell off and my foot was caught in the stirrup. I was being dragged along and was trying to climb back on the horse. The terrified animal was going faster and faster, and I knew I would die. I prayed I would be saved and my angel came to me.

A very short way ahead was a big road with trucks going along and the horse was heading straight for it. Then suddenly the horse ran up into a huge pile of snow and that stopped him. I know it was my guardian angel that had saved me.

Another time, when I was 19 or 20, I was driving my car too fast in the centre of town. I skidded and went right into a wall. The car went in slow motion and stopped exactly at the wall but did not touch the wall. It was as though the angel had enfolded the car. As it was happening, I saw a picture of my face smashed and pouring with blood. Then it did not happen. To this day I can only say time stopped and my angel was there.

My angel protected me again when I was 26. I was driving along with my ex-wife, Elva. It was snowing and she needed to go to the hospital. I was not driving fast, but suddenly a big truck pulled out in front of me and could not stop. I tried to stop the car, but the truck smashed into my car and totally destroyed my side of it. Elva was fine. I was taken to hospital but was not badly hurt. The newspaper reported my miracle escape and said that angels had saved me because I should have been killed, whereas I was able to get out of the car door.

WORKING WITH GUARDIAN AND HEALING ANGELS

Charlotte lives in Ontario. She told me this when I met her, years before I knew much about spirituality, but I have never forgotten her story.

> *I was very unhappy as a child. My mother left home when I was five and my father, a very bitter man, worked long hours and I spent a lot of time alone. The apartment where we lived was on the fourth floor and I had to go in a metal elevator, like a cage. I was always scared it would stop and fall and one day it did lurch and stop mid-floor. I started to cry for my Mom. Suddenly I was picked up and hugged by this big laughing angel. I felt the feather wings and the soft dress. 'We'll fix this,' she said, and pressed the button and it started and stopped at my floor. I got out and the lift went down, but no sound. I wasn't scared ever again in the elevator. However, I never saw her again.*
>
> *After that my Dad met someone nice and we were a family again.*

Julia, who now lives in central France, met her angel when she was hopelessly lost trying to find her new rented home. Her baby, Gemma, was crying in the back of the car. She stopped at a crossroads and a middle-aged woman with a beautiful though wrinkled face appeared from nowhere. Surprisingly, she understood Julia's poor French and explained the directions in English. Julia turned to comfort the baby, and when she turned back, the woman was gone. Incredibly, Julia realised she had not even named the village, still an hour away. Afterwards, Julia described how she seemed to follow a pathway of sunshine and just knew the way.

Julia has felt her angel with her many times during minor crises – when the fire wouldn't light or her old car wouldn't start – and always things turned out well.

I met Julia on the plane from Limoges when she was going home to see her family in England. I mentioned my angel book to her as we chatted about our jobs. Julia is a graphic designer, but she says she can never draw her angel, though she has tried many times and can still see her face ten years later.

Don't worry if you find making contact with your angel hard at first. Take it a step at a time and remain open but not impatient. Your personal angel will slow down and let you catch up, but in the meantime will keep you safe in small ways as well as big ones, and you will have the sense of being cared for.

How do you see your guardian angel?

For some people, their angel is a traditional figure with white robes, golden wings and a golden halo (in fact the aura, or radiant energy field, of the angel, seen most around the head). For others, the angel is a sphere of light or colours, or like the sun shining through early morning mist across a field of snow.

Susanne, who lives in central Sweden, describes her angel like this:

My blue angel is just a blue colour in the shape of an angel with wings, with no specific face but definitely an angel. My angel can become any size according to how scared I am or the kind of help I need.

When I was frightened, sick or just could not cope, I would ask for help and call him, and then I would see the turquoise-blue colour. I am very scared of flying. When I went to Australia, Greece and Spain, I couldn't show the children how frightened I was. My angel lay on the plane and held its body in his huge wings.

Once, when there was a bad storm and high winds at home, I was afraid, but I could feel him holding the house steady with his wings, and we had no damage. I was first aware of my blue angel – definitely male – when I lived in the south of Sweden and had just had my first son. Once my second son, Lucas, was born, years later, my blue angel did not come any more. I believe Lucas is now my blue angel.

Paul, from Lincolnshire, England, describes his angel as definitely male, like a warrior. He sees a flash like glinting steel and feels a sharpness like biting on a lemon. His angel comes to him when he is driving at night, which he has to do quite frequently, and especially if he is feeling tired.

Hilary, from Queensland, Australia, sees her angel when she is working in the early morning on the ward where she is a senior nurse – often when she is feeling tired and dispirited. Her angel comes as light beams that form and re-form. Hilary calls her angel Rebekkah, a name that came into her mind in a soft melodious voice.

Melanie, who lives in Texas, USA, doesn't see her angel but recognises her nonetheless:

My angel comes always with the fragrance of lilies, even when I am in the middle of town, and I feel as though my face is being brushed with a feather. I do not know her name but I feel her when I am about to do something stupid.

Stillness within, stress without

You will most easily connect with your guardian angel's energies if you can spend time in sacred buildings looking at the beautiful carved wood and stone angels, or in art galleries looking at paintings of the heavenly hosts.

When I was writing a book on labyrinths, I visited several medieval cathedrals in France and saw many wonderful angels, some gold, some richly coloured, some painted wooden statues, some sculpted. In Bayeux Cathedral, in northern France, there are medieval fresco angels in the crypt – splendid angels playing bagpipes, an accordion and even a bombard (a flute-type instrument popular in that region of France). In Amiens Cathedral there is a seated stone angel statue on a pillar, called *The Weeping Cherub*, a small chubby infant angel who weeps for the sorrows of the world. When I went to the cathedral in the early morning, sunlight was filtering in through the brilliantly coloured stained-glass window and the cherub was covered with rainbows. To me, these tiny infant angels represent all those who die in infancy or childhood and who become angels because of their innocence and purity, keeping watch over small children and babies in the world.

If, however, great cathedrals and art galleries are inaccessible to you, except on special occasions, you can create your moments of angelic stillness in less idyllic settings. By using your imagination you can create a special space even on a crowded bus or train or in a busy office. Here you and your guardian angel can spend five minutes together. So whenever life gets too much ...

O Stop. Leave everything for five minutes.

O Put your yelling child in a safe, comfortable place, switch off your computer and phone – mobiles especially intrude into every second of consciousness.

O Sit with your feet on the ground and your hands by your sides or resting on chair arms.

O Visualise a rose garden or a quiet sunlit church and merge any everyday sounds into fountains flowing or the hum of bees.

O With the outstretched fingers of each hand, trace around yourself, about an arm-span each side, the shape of an angel, including the wings. If you are in a public place you can pretend you are stretching.

O Trace the angelic halo about three fingers' breadth above and around your head. Say either aloud or in your mind:

> *I call my angel in the middle of this chaos and stress. Come to me;*
> *enclose me in your soft wings. Enter my heart and calm my mind.*
> *Nothing can harm, nothing disturb when you are near. I take the*
> *angel within.*

O Return your hands to your sides and breathe, softly and slowly sighing out each breath and letting any panic, anxiety or stress flow away downwards through your hands and feet.

O Stand up, shake your fingers all around you and picture purple and pink light entering you and spiralling in soft, swirling light beams.

O Let your angel energy flow into the chaos and noise and watch it melt away.

O If possible, set a small crystal angel near your workplace or keep one in a tiny drawstring bag so you can carry it to continue the connection.

Let your guardian angel empower you

That's all very well, you may say, but what if you have three young children screaming with tiredness, an urgent phone call you have to make, your computer has just corrupted the assignment you've been working on all day, the washing machine is flooding the floor and your husband is bringing home five overseas guests for a meal in an hour? What has this to do with angels?

Everything. Of course, angels aren't an on-demand 24/7 fixing service for every crisis life throws at us. If you have a busy life, then you will almost certainly have any number of these moments. When angels do help us through these times with a near-miracle it is a bonus. But the most important power of angels is to empower us so we ourselves can cope with the bad days, the frankly awful days, and those times when all you want to do is to hide under the duvet and howl with frustration. They can bring out our own inner strengths and survival instincts and our superhuman powers to come through, if not smiling, at least still standing.

If you have no time even to hold crystal angels or picture light, you can still call on your guardian angel to help calm you and bring out your inner strength.

O   Stand still for a moment and simply say, with conviction:

I can cope. I will cope. One step at a time, one thing at a time.
Angels come to my aid and help me to help myself.

O   Then take one thing at a time. Deal with the situation decisively, second by second, without allowing yourself to think 'What if ...?' or 'I can't'.

O   Focus on now and tell yourself that you can sort out the mess and it will not go on for ever. Accept that everything may not be perfect, but the guests will enjoy a take-away just as much as a home-cooked meal if they are in welcoming company.

O   Push away everything that is not that one task in hand by visualising a strong breeze blowing all obstructions out of your path.

O   Keep saying, in your mind or aloud softly:

I can cope. I will cope. One step at a time.

You will find that as the panic recedes, so your ingenuity and resourcefulness increase – and when you have won through, you will really feel powerful and harmonious.

Assume that people will be glad to help – it gives them a chance to connect with their angels and awaken their higher energies. Galvanise into action the inert heap of teenagers watching the Cartoon Channel as the water laps round their feet, the neighbour who said 'Any time ...' after you gave him a lift to the station when the early-morning taxi failed to show up.

Be confident that everything will be fixed before long and you will get back on course. So maybe an angel won't come down with a five-course home-cooked meal and a toolbox. But you will find the Off switch for the water or a neighbour with a spanner who knows how to replace the washer. The younger children can go to bed unwashed and watch a video for once. The urgent phone call will just have to wait until the next day – was it really that urgent anyway? The file on the computer can be quickly reconstructed tomorrow, which is blissfully far away. And the overseas guests will get a glimpse of real family life and the joys of choosing their own supper from the local takeaway, washed down with copious glasses of wine.

The more we trust our angels, the more our own power and inner coping mechanisms increase. And we can take most from higher sources when we are resourceful. Above all, as we help others in our earthly path, so blessings pour down on us threefold from cosmic sources and from those around us.

Dream letters

When we are in the realms of sleep, we can most easily receive wisdom from angelic realms. This is because our conscious mind and senses are relaxed and so our spiritual senses, which vibrate at a less material level when the conscious mind is not in control, move closer to angelic vibrations. This brings clear communication.

Dream letters – also known as dream incubation – are a very ancient tradition from Ancient Egyptian and Greek sources, which passed into angel lore in the Middle Ages. Writing night-time letters is a great way of communicating with your guardian angel – either simply to talk or to get answers to any questions you might have. You can use this technique weekly or whenever you have a question or feel you are stuck in the material world and its limitations. The key is to prepare as you would for meeting any special friend.

O Keep a special pen and paper as you did for automatic writing (you can use the same one for both), with green ink if possible.

O Spend the evening quietly and avoid watching stimulating television or working late. Rather, relax by listening to a talking book, a meditation or relaxation tape, or soft music and allow your inner imagery to unfold. Children see angels precisely because their minds operate mainly through pictures that don't limit us, as words do, to specifics.

O Have a bath or slow, warm shower in a bathroom illuminated with purple, soft blue or pink scented nightlights. In the semi-darkness picture soft, coloured mists and swirls, and in your mind angelic images may form. Visualise any tensions or negative feelings from the day washing away down the plug hole.

O Dry yourself and put on something warm and loose, such as a dressing gown. If you normally have a hot drink, make one, and then light more scented candles in your bedroom – or, if you prefer, go to your angel place. Place a pen and paper and a soft reading light by your bed, so you can write down any

49

dreams immediately you awake. We only recall those dreams from which we do wake, and all too easily the content fades, especially if the dream is in the middle of the night.

○ Begin writing and let the words flow. Though a dream letter is not a psychic shopping list for your angel to deliver by morning, you can write about your hopes and fears, your private concerns, your family worries – and especially about your dreams for the future. Ask any specific questions that are troubling you.

○ When you have finished, touch your hairline and say softly three times:

Above me the light.

○ Then touch the centre of your brow and say three times even more quietly:

Within me the radiance.

○ Touch the centre of your throat. Say even more softly three times:

To receive the wise truth.

○ Finally, touch your heart and whisper three times:

Deep in my heart.

○ Fold the letter and put it in an unmarked envelope beneath your pillow. Some people keep a small scented cushion cover for such letters. Blow out the candles and lie down, visualising again the swirling colours. You may smell a fragrance deeper and richer than that of the scented candles, which in time you will recognise as your angel's unique fragrance. But if not, it does not mean your angel is not present, rather that you connect in other ways.

○ Recite the angel protection words above as you drift into sleep, and picture an angel walking through the mist towards you.

○ Even if you do not dream of your angel, you may be aware of a rich light in your dream. Some have described this as like being enclosed in a ring of radiance. Your dreams will be more vivid and the symbols more memorable and significant on waking.

○ When you awake in the morning, even if no specific images or symbols came, you will feel refreshed and optimistic, and the solutions to your question will unfold during the day spontaneously.

○ In the evening, sit by candlelight and re-read your dream records, re-creating the scenes in your imagination. You may realise instantly how clearly your questions have been answered. If not, allow the meanings of the symbols to unfold slowly or look them up in a dream dictionary. Often we may see a dream symbol in the most unlikely circumstances the following day as confirmation that the dream and symbol had special significance.

O Keep your dream letters in a special box, locked if you have no privacy, tied with pink ribbon. When the box is full, burn the letters in a fire scented with pine or sage.

You can also use the four phrases from this ritual – in your mind or aloud – touching the four points as you think or say them, whenever you want to feel your angel close. I have sometimes spoken the words when alone on a station late at night or in an unfamiliar city as darkness falls. Recently I was staying in Stockholm, Sweden, in a lovely hotel near the station. I had been to visit a New Age bookstore. On my way back I saw a church I had read about in my tourist guide and walked off the main street in the deep snow to explore. Then I realised that a group of young male drug addicts was gathered in the deserted churchyard. One of them came towards me menacingly and tried to reach out to me. I said the angel chant rather than panicking, and kept walking. He backed away and I returned to the street. It may have been coincidence; it may have been the confidence I was giving off, as all fear left me with the words – my angel helping me to help myself. Whatever the case, what might have been an unfortunate incident was averted.

Household guardian angels

We usually have one household guardian angel per family, whether the family consists of a single person living alone or several generations sharing a house. These angels tend to offer practical forms of assistance. They may help when you are worried about security issues, are having a lot of minor accidents in your home or are exhausted but have to care for a family and work for a living without much earthly support. Household angels are remarkably good at assisting your guardian angel when you hit a domestic crisis.

Jacky Newcomb is the author of a book called *The Angel Treasury* (Element, 2005). But before she knew about angels she was another struggling mother. Jacky told me:

> *My youngest daughter, Georgina, was suffering from a very sick stomach, and clean sheets were at a premium. Every time my head hit the pillow she called out for help.*
>
> *'Mama,' she cried out, for what seemed like the hundredth time. Wearily I got out of bed to change yet another pair of sheets. After an hour or more of jumping out of bed (and running out of bedding) I came up with idea of making my daughter up a bed of towels in the bathroom. I was so exhausted that I was ready to try anything. Safe in the belief that she would be able to reach the toilet to be sick now, I got back into bed, only to be woken again moments later.*

Frustrated and tired, I walked to the bathroom. My daughter lay with sweat dripping down her face, and I felt mean and wanted someone to blame. I remembered the angel books I'd been reading and yelled out crossly: 'If there is such a thing as angels, then YOU come and look after her now! I am too tired to do this any more!' And I'm ashamed to say that I also swore to myself.

My reply came in the most unexpected way. Suddenly, the bathroom was filled with music. The sound of a large orchestra seemed to come from within the room itself! Feeling confused, I looked around for an explanation. Finding none, I stepped over my daughter and into the bath so that I could open the bathroom window and peek out to the fields at the back of the house. It seemed more logical that a band might be playing in the fields than that some unseen spiritual guardians were trumpeting my reply! Naturally, there was nothing outside – it was after midnight!

Was the sound coming from the rest of the house, I wondered? Cautiously I checked the rest of the house, but the sound was definitely coming from within the bathroom itself.

I realised that I'd called for angels and angels had come to help. I had to accept that the most obvious explanation was now the only one. I looked down at my daughter so that I could share the moment with her, but she was sleeping soundly.

Georgina slept right through until the morning, and when she woke she was fine. She has no memory of the night at all but firmly believes in angels just the same.

Household angels, if seen at all, are usually surrounded by a rich green or golden brown glow, sometimes with sparks of golden light and slowly circling rainbows (even in a room where there is no obvious light reflection). They are most easily perceived in the early morning or evening. They may be accompanied by soft music – sometimes resembling a musical box sound – even when there is no obvious source of music. We may occasionally mistake these angels for ghosts or household elves or gnomes who care for and protect the home. But household angels' energies are always warm and benign, still and flowing. They bring a sense of peace, and even animals and children will become quiet and calm as they connect with the domestic angelic power.

Household angels are more attached to the family than to the building and may move with them, though very old houses may have their own guardians. When individual children set up their own homes or a person leaves the family, a new angel will follow them to help them settle.

Household angels are ruled by Gabriel, Archangel of the Moon. He emits silver rays like soft moonlight. His special crystal is the moonstone and his incense myrrh or lemon verbena.

Making an angelic heart of the home

In the previous chapter we created an angel place within the home, and you can, of course, talk to your household angel there. However, that is your private place, so you might like to set up a small household angel place at the centre of your home. Though your household angel is always present, by making an angelic place you can concentrate and spread the energies throughout the household. If you move into a new house that seems unfriendly or impersonal or you are in temporary accommodation or living in less than ideal circumstances, this ritual can be especially helpful.

○ Choose a small flat surface and place on it a golden yellow or deep green pot plant (living plants are better than cut flowers for angel places).

○ In the centre of the surface place a bowl of yellow and orange fruit, such as apples, oranges and bananas, and a dish of dried fruits and seeds or tiny golden candies. Offer these to visitors to spread the joy.

○ Place a golden rutilated quartz, carnelian, red tiger's eye or tiny piece of amber at each of the four corners to concentrate the energies. You need only use small crystals.

○ If you like, you can add a small circle of moonstones and burn one of Gabriel's incenses before you go to bed every Sunday to invoke his protection of the home for the week ahead.

○ Once a week, light a beeswax or yellow candle and sit quietly (with children or your partner if you have them) looking into the candlelight and talking over the previous week. This can be a good Friday night connection after a busy week. You can share experiences, talk about small domestic worries and make plans for the weekend and the future. But choose a night that suits you.

○ You might like to incorporate a meal of simple yellow and golden foods, baked potatoes, a vegetable soup and golden bread, or a meat casserole. Let the youngest member of the family ask the household angel for a special blessing on the meal.

Household angels do not expect a lot of fuss or ritual, but keep your household angel place tidy and fresh. As a result, the energies will spread calm through your house all week long.

Healing angels

As well as our guardian angel, we have other angels around us at different times in our lives. Among these are the healing angels, who help us not only in healing ourselves but also in healing those we love.

Most of the personal healing angels who work with us never tell us their names, although you can ask by using the method suggested on pages 29–30 for discovering the identity of your guardian angel. The four most important healing angels are:

Raphael: The supreme Archangel of Spiritual and Physical Healers and Healing, leader of all the healing angels. He carries a traveller's staff and is surrounded by pure green light. His incense is lavender and his crystal is yellow citrine or malachite. He is assisted by Ariel, Anael and Zadkiel.

Ariel: The Archangel who heals animals and nature, his name means 'Lion of God'. A golden-yellow light surrounds him. His incense is patchouli and his crystal moss agate or jade.

Anael (or Haniel): The Archangel of healing remedies and crystal healing. He is surrounded by rose-pink light. His incense is rose and his crystals rose quartz or pink chalcedony.

Zadkiel: The most gentle of Archangels, good with children and all who are depressed or afraid. He is surrounded by pale blue light. His incense is chamomile and his crystals are angelite or blue chalcedony.

Working with healing angels

Generally, our personal healing angels are characterised by a green- or rose-coloured light – or sometimes a very pale blue. They have rather 'spacey', floating energies and are often surrounded by a mist that is warm and quite dry. You may first become aware of them when you are sick and alone, or when you are caring for small children and really need some instant healing power when no earthly help is available.

I met my healing angel during a storm that broke while I was staying alone in my remote caravan. The electricity failed and my mobile phone was out of signal because of the weather. It was late October and the caravan site was almost deserted.

I suffer from gall bladder problems and was having a bad attack. In the dark I could not find my painkillers. Like an idiot, though I had plenty of candles, I had run out of matches. I wasn't in danger but I was in pain and felt totally and utterly wretched. I just lay there, scared of the darkness and the fierce storm. I didn't even have the energy to call upon an angel.

Suddenly, I was aware of a pale but warm blue mist around me. I felt that I was being rocked rhythmically like a child, very gently. The feeling was totally different from the swaying and banging of the metal caravan in the high wind. I closed my eyes and the pain ebbed away, as did my fear. I felt totally at peace and fell into a deep sleep. When I woke, it was light and the storm had gone.

Later, when I told my good friend and wise healer Lilian about the experience, she said: 'Oh, that was Carina, the blue healing angel. She always rocks people like a mother when they are in pain.'

I haven't been able to find any reference to Carina, but I know she was there for me that night.

Healing angels shouldn't be called for every ache and pain or to act as a substitute for conventional medical care. However, they are wonderful if you are exhausted, distressed or in pain that won't go away even after medication. We can all ask our healing angel to help us heal ourselves, our family and our friends, whether they are absent or present. Afterwards you or the person you are helping will generally experience a sense of peace and relief. You may see pink, green or blue mists, and your own self-healing system will kick into action. For even in healing, angels help us to help ourselves, albeit unconsciously.

If you do healing work, you may already be aware of your healing angel – or angels, for some people have more than one. If you say a silent prayer before beginning therapy you can often connect with your patient's angel as well, who will help their body to accept the healing. We will be talking more about prayer in Chapter 6.

Just one note of caution ... While it can never be wrong to send angelic light to someone with an illness of any kind, however serious, you cannot and should not make any promises of recovery. Sometimes all we can do is ask our healing angel and that of the sick person to join and give healing if they can, and if they cannot, just to bring relief and ease.

Making healing angel waters

One of the best ways to channel the healing of the angels is by making angel waters. These are waters in which one of the healing angel crystals has been soaked. These crystals are:

○ Angelite

○ Blue lace agate

○ Blue or pink chalcedony

○ Rose quartz – or the rarer manganocalcite, a special soft pink form of polished calcite

In angel healing the blue crystals are the energisers and the pink ones the soothers of pain, anxiety and tension, so you can make energising and soothing waters separately and mix them if and when necessary. Pink waters are also excellent for women in childbirth and all mothers under stress.

Ideally you should make your angel waters on the night when you first see the crescent moon in the sky. She is first seen in the western sky during the later afternoon and early evening. However, a night or two after the first crescent is good enough. Of course, if you need angel water and it is the wrong moon phase, your healing angel will empower it at any time.

○ First wash the crystals well under running water.

55

○ Use a clear glass jug (not plastic or metal) for each kind of water. Set in each jug three small crystals, blue in the one jug and pink in the other.

○ Add a litre (2 pints) of still mineral or filtered water – or tap water if it is pure in your area – to each jug.

○ Cover each jug with a clear lid or plate made of any material (do not use clingfilm, because this is not a natural product) and set the two jugs side by side on an indoor window ledge, facing the west if possible. The blue crystal jug should be to the left and the pink to the right. If you leave home early, you can set the water in the morning before you go out.

○ You are now going to make the sign of the cross in the air over the top of each jug in turn, completing the first cross before moving on to the second jug. You will be drawing each of the four arms of the cross separately. First draw the downward arm of the cross as far as the centre of the top of the blue jug and say:

> *Wise Raphael, Archangel of all healers and of healing, bless this water*
> *and bring healing to all it touches if it is right to be.*

Picture Raphael's green rays entering the water.

○ Then make the right-to-left horizontonal to meet the vertical Raphael line and say:

Zadkiel, gentle Archangel who loves children and all who are depressed or afraid, bless this water and bring healing to all it touches if it is right to be.

Picture Zadkiel's pale blue rays entering the water.

○ Make the upward vertical arm of the cross in the air to meet the Raphael one and say:

> *Loving Ariel, Archangel of animal healing and restorer of spoilt nature,*
> *bless this water and bring healing to all it touches if it is right to be.*

See Ariel's golden-yellow light entering the water.

○ Finally, make the left to right horizontal line to complete the air cross, saying:

> *Kind Anael, Archangel of healing wisdom and of crystal healing,*
> *bless this water and bring healing to all it touches if it is right to be.*

See the rose light filtering into the jug.

○ Repeat the words and actions over the pink water jug.

○ Set either four clear small crystal angels or four purple amethyst or purple fluorite crystals in a square to enclose both jugs and leave them from mid-morning to early evening (or till you can no longer see the moon in the sky if

WORKING WITH GUARDIAN AND HEALING ANGELS

it is a clear evening). If you are using a different moon time, check in a newspaper or diary for moonrise and set.

○ The water is now ready to be used. Filter it from the jugs and keep it in small clear bottles with screw-top lids or, if you can obtain them, blue and pink (or red) glass bottles. Keep the pink and blue angel healing crystals in a safe place for next time.

Using healing angel waters

There are many possible uses for healing angel waters. You can add a few drops to baths and drinks, splash it on pulse points and the brow, or on any crystals or a pendulum you are using in healing.

To heal sick animals and birds add a little of the water to their normal drinking water every day for a week. If you are using the water to heal someone else (be they animal or human), as you work, ask your personal healing angel to send his or her power to assist you and help whoever you are healing to recover if it is right to be.

If a person is sick or distressed, you can sprinkle the water at the four corners of their bed and ask their healing angel to enfold them. This is particularly good for children – and is also a good way of helping you to sleep if you are troubled.

You can send absent healing (to those who are not physically present), to both people and animals, by sprinkling droplets of the two waters mixed in a small glass bowl round a picture of the subject. Make a clockwise circle of water droplets three times, naming the subject, the illness and asking your healing angel to send light. You can also heal places by this method, sprinkling the water around a picture of an endangered or war-torn place.

Ask your angel for healing

With time and experience you can dispense with rituals and waters and simply ask your healing angel, in your mind, for healing – for yourself or for another.

○ Hold your palms upwards and allow your angel's rays to flow into them. These rays may be green, pink or blue – or perhaps a mixture of all three. You will know the colour from the work you have done with your angel.

○ After two or three minutes, you will feel the warmth of your healing angel passing into your hands, up your arms and into your heart, and then back down your arms into your hands in a continuing cycle.

○ If you are healing another, allow your hands to move naturally, tracing their own pattern, two or three centimetres (an inch or so) from the patient. You can pause and hold your hand close to any obviously painful place on the body and let the power flow till you sense it is time to move on. Trust the angel to guide your movements.

○ If you wish, you can use two round crystals, one soft blue and one pink, to facilitate healing. These should be kept in a soft cloth pouch when they are not in use. Hold the blue crystal in your power hand (the one you write with) and the pink one in the other hand, allowing them to trace their own path over your own or your patient's energy paths until you feel the pain or tension leave and energy return. I often move the blue crystal clockwise and the pink one anticlockwise. But trust yourself and your angel, and your hands will be gently guided exactly on the right path – just as a wise adult guides the hand of a much-loved child.

○ As you continue to work, you may notice the angel colours becoming gradually clearer. You may even see a misty form standing at your side, while another supports the patient from behind.

○ Five minutes is usually enough for a healing session. You will know the healing is complete when you feel the heat subsiding. If you are using crystals, they will slow down and then stop.

○ Wash the crystals under running water to cleanse them and replace them in their pouch. Thank your own angel and your patient's.

If you call on your healing angel for help at any time informally – when you are hugging a sad friend, rubbing the brow of a partner with a headache or allowing the angel's energy to relieve you after a hard day – your hands will become warm and tingle as the angelic power flows through you.

6

Archangels

In this chapter we will be working with the Archangels to draw their spiritual qualities into our lives and move spiritually upwards. We will also be connecting with the energies of the higher choirs of angels. Though I refer to the Archangels as 'he', they are in fact, as I have already said, androgynous, and some people see Gabriel and Anael as having a more female focus.

Archangels may seem more remote than our guardian angels because they are not daily visitors in our lives. However, they can intervene at critical moments and offer great personal comfort, as the two following accounts, both relating to Michael, show. Catherine, who lives in the north of England, told me:

> My mother Norah had always been terrified of dying. A few days before Christmas 1991, Mum was told that she had a large tumour on her brain and that her condition was very serious.

On 27 December, Norah was in hospital, alone and afraid, awaiting a major operation the next morning. She continues the story:

> It was late at night. I said: 'Oh, Michael, protect me!'
> He came with the faintest of sounds. He was so beautiful, about eight feet (6.6 metres) tall with ash blonde hair, just above his shoulders. He was wearing a cream full-length robe, edged at the neck with gold. Michael was not at all feminine. He was so strong but with the most beautiful face I have ever seen in my life. In his hand he held a magnificent sword, enormous and very heavy, yet he raised it as though it was no heavier than a feather. Michael gestured to me with his hand to go behind him and then he opened his wings slightly. The feathers were like the softest down and cream, edged with apricot. He closed his wings around me and I knew I was safe. Then he was gone, but since that night I have never been frightened and I have felt full of peace.

Catherine was amazed by the transformation in her mother. She relates:

> The morning of the operation, we went with my mother to the operating theatre. She needed no pre-medication. She smiled and waved to us as we left her, and she survived the seven-hour operation. The brain tumour was found to be malignant, and we were told there was nothing more to be done. However, after her

experience with Michael, she never again knew fear. Mum was smiling when she died.

Archangels can also act as protectors during birth. Carol, an editor, from Santa Fe, New Mexico, USA, describes how in her second stage of labour, the birth just seemed to stop:

After three hours I was exhausted and a sense of fear and hopelessness was affecting us all. My midwife was especially tired, having been up all the previous night birthing my friend's baby.

There was a clear pause between pains. I stood up on the bed. I felt strength filling me as I asked for help from Michael, a being I have experienced through all my life as a guide and protector. The fear disappeared, the room was filled with light and suddenly everyone sprang into action. I managed to push the baby (who was lying on her back) so that the midwife could carefully manoeuvre her out.

My daughter was born safely within minutes, and I named her Mikhaila, for I am convinced Michael intervened to save her. Even three weeks after the birth, friends commented on the holy atmosphere in our home.

Though I was aware of other birth angels around me, it was Michael who came to my aid.

What are the Archangels?

Archangels represent archetypal or idealised qualities. Don't worry if you read about the militaristic qualities of Archangels in biblical writings. These come from the early need to defend the established faiths against unbelievers and those who still followed earlier Mother Goddess religions or religions with many deity forms. Similarly, as I mentioned earlier, the concept of dark, or fallen, Archangels arose as an attempt to explain how evil could exist. Thus the theory arose of a war between angels. But this is just a theory. Archangels and angels are always good. Even Satan, or the devil, was originally Lucifer, Archangel of Light, who was demonised to explain why bad things happen in the world.

There are many more Archangels than are mentioned in this book – you may like to do your own research and write about them in your angel journal. The names of many of the Archangels are given in different forms in different religious traditions. I have given some of these variations in the section on each Archangel.

As I mentioned on page 38, in spite of their elevated roles in the seven heavens, Archangels are concerned with our spiritual welfare. They assist us to aspire beyond purely personal concerns. However, they will also help with our difficulties. Archangels are a particularly useful source of help when you need a lot of power or sudden urgent aid. Simply call on the appropriate one.

Of course, you can link personal problems with global ones. Thus you could appeal to the Archangel of compassion, Cassiel, to aid nations struggling with crippling debt. As a result of your prayers for others, you would be helped with any private debt problems relating to yourself and your family.

Archangel assistance, however, may not be easy to receive. Karen, from Hampshire, England, a sound healer, comments that Archangel energies aren't soft and at times can feel uncomfortable and challenging, as they force us to examine how our own attitudes or inertia contribute to what we may have perceived as purely external trials and obstacles.

In some ways it is easier to visualise an Archangel than an individual guardian, because there are a number of descriptions of the Archangels, drawn from different sources, to guide us. These indicate not only each individual Archangel's appearance but also the areas they govern and their associated crystals, candle colours and so on.

Keep a page in your angel journal for each Archangel and note down any information you come across, whether on the internet, in churches or cathedrals, in art galleries, or during your own rituals or moments of quiet contemplation. Over time, you may evolve your own concept of the Archangels – quite possibly one that is entirely different from that of traditional lore. If it works for you, trust your own insights. Archangels, like angels, are made of pure energy and light, and so we give them their earthly form, according to how we perceive them.

The four main Archangels

We have most information about the four Archangels who are central to angelology, Gabriel, Michael, Raphael and Uriel.

Gabriel

Direction: West

Season: Autumn

Time of day: Sunset

Day: Monday

Planet: Moon

Colour: Silver

Incenses: Eucalyptus, jasmine, lemon verbena, lily, myrrh, lilac, rose

Crystals: Aquamarine, aqua aura, moonstone, milky quartz, opal, pearls, selenite

Element: Water

Metal: Silver

Gabriel is the second-highest of the Archangels (after Michael). His name means 'God has shown himself mightily'. Archangel Gabriel carries God's messages and reveals the answers to the questions we carry deep in our hearts.

Gabriel was herald to Elizabeth, telling her that though long past childbearing age she would give birth to John the Baptist. He also took the news to Mary that she would have a son, Jesus. He chooses the souls of children to be born and teaches them in the nine months their spirits move between the mother and the heavens. When the child is born, Gabriel presses his finger on its face so that the child will keep the secrets of the heavens, so creating the cleft below the nose.

Gabriel is pictured in silver or the blue of the night sky, with a mantle of stars and a crescent moon for his halo. He wears a golden horn and carries a white lily or a lantern in his right hand and a mirror made of jasper in his left.

Gabriel is the patron of the household; of communications and postal workers; of all in the hotel or hospitality trade; of market researchers; dieticians; conference planners; secretaries; desktop publishers; family physicians; women's aid workers and translators.

Invoke Gabriel for protection against inclement weather; for travel across water; for matters concerning women; for diminishing self-destructive tendencies; to protect water creatures and to cleanse polluted seas, lakes and rivers.

Michael

Direction: South

Season: Summer

Time of day: Noon

Day: Sunday

Planet: Sun

Colour: Gold

Incenses: Chamomile, frankincense, marigold, rosemary, sunflower, sage

Crystals: Amber, clear quartz crystal, Herkimer diamond, opal or angel aura, golden topaz

Element: Fire

Metal: Gold

Michael, whose name means 'Who is like to God', is the supreme Archangel. He oversees the natural world, the weather and the growth of crops. He is the leader of all the great warrior angels who fight against evil and he is often shown trampling the devil underfoot. Michael appeared to Moses as the fire in the burning bush and rescued Daniel from the lion's den.

Michael is pictured with golden wings, in red and gold armour, with a sword, a shield and a green date branch. He carries the scales of justice or a white banner with a red cross. He is the ideal golden-haired young warrior and is one of the chief dragon-slaying angels. In Muslim lore, his wings are said to be the colour of green emeralds.

Michael is the patron of grocers; sailors; administrators; car repairers and garage mechanics; railway workers; police officers; mechanical engineers; lorry drivers; construction engineers and builders and metalworkers.

Invoke Michael for abundance and prosperity; leadership; focus; striving for perfection (what the alchemists called spiritual gold); reviving barren land despoiled by industrialisation; and cleansing the air of pollution.

Raphael

Direction: East

Season: Spring

Time of day: Dawn

Day: Wednesday

Planet: Mercury

Colour: Lemon yellow or misty grey, but often also perceived as green

Incenses: Lavender, lily of the valley, pine and thyme

Crystals: Citrine, yellow and orange calcite, yellow jasper, golden beryl, lemon chrysoprase

Element: Air

Metal: Aluminium, mercury

Raphael, whose name means 'God has healed', is the Archangel of the four winds, science, medicine and all forms of healing. He showed Noah how to build the Ark and then, after the Flood, healed the earth and gave Noah a medical book. He also healed the blind Tobit in the Holy Scriptures.

Raphael takes care of the blind and of travellers, especially those who are young and vulnerable and far from home. He presides over joyful meetings and celebrations. In the Old Testament, he gave King Solomon a magical ring to help him in the building of his great temple.

Picture Raphael carrying a golden vial of medicine and a traveller's staff, with food (often a fish) in his wallet to nourish travellers. He is dressed in the colours of early-morning sunlight, with a beautiful green healing ray emanating from his halo.

Raphael is patron of nurses; physicians; shopkeepers; bus drivers; technicians; scientists; healthcare workers; travellers; all who work in technology – especially

63

software production; tour operators; the self-employed; youth workers; taxi drivers; chiropractors and packers.

Invoke Raphael for healing and health; business ventures; technological issues; science; travel to places near or far; buying and selling; issues to do with books; neighbourhood matters; and against technological and chemical pollution and the adverse effects of modern living.

Uriel

Direction: North

Season: Winter

Time of day: Midnight

Day: Tuesday

Planet: Mars

Colour: Ruby red

Incenses: Basil, copal, sandalwood and ginger

Crystals: Hematite, obsidian, rutilated quartz and tiger's eye

Metal: Burnished gold, brass

Uriel, whose name means 'Fire of God', is the Archangel of Transformation. Uriel is a regent, or guardian, of the sun and the sharpest-sighted Archangel in heaven. He is the Archangel who brought alchemy to humankind. Alchemy is the sacred art of transmuting base metal into gold, a process intended to refine spirit as well as matter and believed to be the way humans can find the way back to paradise. He guards the gates of the Garden of Eden with his fiery sword until we are wise enough to return.

Uriel warned Noah of the Flood. He is a pillar of pure fire and brings warmth to the winter, melting the snows with his flaming sword.

Picture Uriel holding a flame in an open hand and bearing a fiery sword. He is dressed in rich, burnished gold and ruby-red, with a bright halo blazing like a bonfire in the darkness.

Uriel is patron of all who undertake creative work; those who relieve disasters; bailiffs; students and teachers; chemists; industrialists; goldsmiths; safety executives; blacksmiths; electrical and gas workers and fire personnel.

Invoke Uriel for protection; for change of all kinds; for the fulfilment of a long-term spiritual path; for quelling anger in others and transforming our own powerful emotions such as fury, jealousy, resentment and spite into impetus for positive change; for focusing ourselves single-mindedly on making the world a better and safer place.

The four subsidiary Archangels

The following four Archangels – Samael, Anael, Sachiel and Cassiel – are the four most commonly used and recognised angels in various sources after the four main Archangels. They are associated with the days of the week and the traditional planets known to early astrologers. Traditionally Archangels number seven to correspond with the seven planets and the days of the week. I have given two for Tuesday and Mars and you can choose which you prefer. Samael tends to be used most in magic lists for Tuesday though Uriel always sits in the north in magic rituals.

- O **Sunday/the sun:** Michael
- O **Monday/the moon:** Gabriel
- O **Tuesday/Mars:** Uriel or Samael
- O **Wednesday/Mercury:** Raphael
- O **Thursday/Jupiter:** Sachiel
- O **Friday/Venus:** Anael
- O **Saturday/Saturn:** Cassiel

Other Archangels are also associated with the days of the week and the planets; these are listed on pages 68–74.

Samael (Sammael)

Day: Tuesday

Planet: Mars

Colour: Red/indigo

Incenses: Allspice, cinnamon, dragon's blood, fern, fig

Crystals: Blood or red agate, garnet, ruby, iron pyrites, titanium aura

Element: Fire

Metal: Iron, steel

Samael is Archangel of Severity, and rules over personal integrity. In place of Uriel, he is usually considered to represent Tuesday and the planet Mars. He is the Archangel of cleansing fire and of overcoming all obstacles in the way of truth. He also protects the home, including our furniture and personal possessions, against thieves and damage by fire or flood.

One of the seven regents of the world and said to be served by two million angels, he is also the so-called Dark Angel, who, in the guise of the serpent, tempted Eve. In this role – which may seem hard to understand at first – he was both a true tester of faith and the revolutionary force that introduced the concept of free will, rather than blind obedience, into the Garden of Eden. He is not necessarily an easy Archangel to work with – and may be one you might like to leave until later in your explorations. He does challenge the status quo and demands that we examine our motives and make our own choices, rather than go along with the way things have always been or the majority view. He insists on integrity and honesty of purpose, so if we do choose to work with him, we may have to do a fair amount of mental cleansing and also take care of our bodies.

Visualise Samael in midnight-blue and red, with midnight-blue wings and blue and red flames in his halo. He sweeps through the skies, waking the slumbering angels and scattering slumbering mortals with a huge, gleaming, dark gold sword.

He is patron of all military personnel; aid workers; peace campaigners; wise politicians and officials at every level; historians; crossword and quiz writers; school and college examiners and inspectors; driving test instructors and examiners and fitness trainers.

Invoke him for all matters where truth is of the essence; for making your own decisions and, if necessary, standing alone for an unpopular cause you believe is right. Call on him also to relieve the suffering of oppressed minorities and endangered species.

Sachiel

Day: Thursday

Planet: Jupiter

Colour: Deep blue and purple

Incenses: Fennel, honeysuckle, lotus, sagebrush

Crystals: Cobalt aura, blue topaz, Angelite, lapis lazuli, sodalite

Element: Air

Metal: Tin

Sachiel, whose name means 'the Covering of God', is called the Divine Benefactor and the Archangel of Charity. He is one of the mighty Cherubim and orders the four elements, Earth, Air, Fire and Water. He has also become associated with good harvests, taking over this role from the pre-Christian corn gods.

Picture Sachiel with a rich purple and golden halo and blue and purple wings. He wears robes of deep blue and purple and carries sheaves of corn and baskets of food.

Sachiel is patron of charity workers; insurance and bank workers; lawyers; bosses; solicitors and judges; agricultural workers; town planners; farmers and supermarket workers.

Invoke Sachiel for good harvests, physical and emotional; for relieving lands where there is famine or disease and restoring rundown areas of cities; for justice and increasing abundance and prosperity for the good of all.

Anael (Hanael/Haniel)

Day: Friday

Planet: Venus

Colour: Rose-pink, green

Incenses: Hibiscus, apple blossom, cherry, rose, strawberry, valerian

Crystals: Green jasper, rose quartz, pink calcite, green fluorite, chrysoprase

Element: Water

Metal: Copper

Anael, whose name means 'Glory or Grace of God', is the Archangel that guards the gates of the West Wind. He took Enoch to the heavenly realms and was one of the seven angels present at creation. He rules over all kingdoms, kings, queens and – more recently – presidents and prime ministers. He is also Archangel of love, healing remedies and crystal healing, and is the Archangel most invoked for gradual growth, be it increase of health, love, good fortune or money.

Picture Anael surrounded by rose-pink and green light, with silver wings and delicate feminine features. His hands are full of flowers, especially roses.

Anael is patron of alternative healers; gardeners and horticulturists; carpenters; daycare centre and pre-school workers; textile workers; mineralologists; counsellors; night workers; call-centre staff; pharmacists; dancers; glaziers; florists and social workers.

Invoke Anael for beauty; love; marriage; the arts; music; the environment; matters concerning children and reconciliation; reforestation; the preservation of mineral resources and earth's natural fuels and for bringing nature into cities.

Cassiel

Day: Saturday

Planet: Saturn

Colour: Indigo, black

Incenses: Cypress, patchouli, mimosa, violet

Crystals: Black onyx, brown jasper, jet, snowflake obsidian, black tourmaline, green aventurine

Element: Earth

Metal: Lead, pewter

Cassiel, whose name means 'he who weeps silently', is known as the angel of tears and solitude. He weeps for the sorrows of the world and also helps to heal them. Some have linked him to the primal darkness before creation. He is Archangel of the mind and of memory, of the expansion of knowledge and of great thinkers. He is also the Archangel of balance who unifies all things, darkness and light, sorrow and joy, night and day. He rules over games of chance and good luck.

Visualise him bearded, with indigo flames sparking from his halo. He rides a dragon and wears dark robes.

Cassiel is patron of estate agents and mortgage brokers; university professors; investors; stockbrokers; architects; inventors; geniuses; gamblers; and those who work with old people and the disabled.

Invoke him for patience; for help with all slow-moving matters and with practical or financial worries that distract you from the path of spirituality. He is also potent for the conservation of natural resources and of traditional values; for relief of chronic pain and loosening of addictions; for matters concerning older people and for all property issues.

The power Archangels

The power Archangels are sources of inspiration and focused energy. Those listed here are my special favourites and are all very accessible through ritual and personal prayer. Each Archangel has special areas of concern and protects members of particular trades or professions.

You can visualise the power Archangels in the ways I have suggested or according to your own personal vision if it is different. The special crystals, candle colours and incenses are listed to assist you to weave your own rituals.

Ariel

Day: Saturday

Planet: Saturn

Colour: Violet

Incenses: Moss, musk, lemon, any fruit incenses

Crystals: All earth jaspers (such as leopardskin and Dalmatian jasper) and agates (such as snakeskin agate, moss agate and tree agate)

Element: Air

Metal: Pewter

Ariel's name means 'Lion of God'. He is called the Keeper of the Sacred Wisdom, Archangel of Mystery and the Guardian of Prophecy. He is the Archangel who heals animals, birds, fish and nature in general, and he is guardian of nature essences and spirits such as fairies and elves. He is one of the seven great angel princes who rule the waters of the heavens and the earth.

Picture Ariel as a middle-aged and masculine in appearance, with long silver hair and eyes that have been described as violet. He is surrounded by yellow light. His cloak is a radiant white that becomes all the colours of the rainbow towards the bottom. He carries a scroll and is sometimes depicted with a lion's head or lion headdress.

Ariel is patron of veterinarians; animal rescue workers; animal breeders and trainers; archaeologists; anthropologists; bartenders; ferry workers; canal and river lockkeepers; civil engineers; forestry workers; plumbers; space scientists; and those who work in laundries and cleaning.

Invoke Ariel for clean water everywhere; for protecting animals against bad living conditions and cruelty; for bringing back a love of nature; for healing the ozone layer; and for developing psychic and prophetic abilities.

Azrael (Asrael/Izra'il)

Day: Tuesday

Planet: Mars

Colour: Deep amethyst

Incenses: A mixture of cedar, juniper and sandalwood (use one stick of each fragrance) or magnolia or any spice

Crystals: Amethyst, purple fluorite, falcon's eye, cat's eye

Element: Earth

Metal: Iron

Azrael is the Archangel of the natural cycles of life and death. He is present at the beginning and end of life, writing in a huge book the name of the person and the time of their birth, and then erasing the name after their earthly life is finished. Death is said to come when a leaf bearing the person's name falls to earth, and Azrael accompanies them on their 40-day journey to heaven.

Azrael is thus both awe-inspiring and protective. He is a giant among Archangels, his feet spanning the heavens. He brought the handful of earth from which Adam was created.

Visualise Azrael with a halo of dark purple flames; huge, dark wings; and an enfolding, deep-red and purple cloak.

Azrael is the patron of anaesthetists; archivists and museum curators; butchers; funeral directors; ambulance drivers and paramedics; workers in the fishing industry and forensic scientists.

Invoke Azrael in times of sorrow; bereavement and all kinds of loss; also at the beginning of any journey – physical or spiritual – and to protect babies; the very young or the very old. He can also help you to sever connections with an old way of life that is not fruitful.

Camael (Chamuel)

Day: Tuesday

Planet: Mars

Colour: Red

Incenses: Ginger, geranium, all mints, parsley, neroli, tangerine

Crystals: Bloodstone, carnelian, fire opal, orange aragonite, red and orange jasper

Element: Fire

Metal: Iron, steel

Camael is known as the Archangel of Courage in Adversity. He is Angel of Divine Love and the patron angel of all who love God. He is a gatekeeper of heaven, protecting souls on their journey after death. He also represents divine justice. According to the Book of Revelations, Camael guards the heavens, holding back the monster Leviathan. In this he is assisted by 12,000 fiery angels. Camael brought strength to Christ in the Garden of Gethsemane before his crucifixion.

Visualise Camael in a deep-red tunic and dark-green armour, with a halo of dark ruby flames and rich green wings. Alternatively, visualise him as a crouching leopard on a rock, which is how he is sometimes depicted.

Camael is patron of surgeons; security guards; peacekeeping forces throughout the world; workers in animal conservation; all who work in traffic control, including air traffic controllers; explosives experts and hairdressers.

Invoke Camael for overcoming war, destruction and adversaries; for guarding the innocent in war-torn lands; for dealing with problems caused by human weakness or negativity; for successful surgery; and whenever you need courage or strength.

Jophiel (Iophiel/Zophiel)

Day: Wednesday

Planet: Mercury

Colour: Deep yellow

Incenses: Ivy, lemongrass, orange, grapefruit

Crystals: Ametrine, rutilated quartz, smoky quartz

Element: Air

Metal: Aluminium, mercury

Jophiel's name means 'Beauty of God'. He is Archangel of Paradise and of Illumination. He is prince of the angelic choir of the Cherubim. Jophiel drove Adam and Eve from the Garden of Eden and, like Uriel, guards the Tree of Knowledge with his fiery sword until humans are sufficiently evolved to use its wisdom with care. He also protected Noah's sons. Jophiel is an angel of joy and has strong female energies.

Picture Jophiel in yellow robes, with an orange, sun-like halo. He radiates sunbeams and has long, yellow hair and pale yellow wings.

Jophiel is patron of advertisers; bakers; carpet fitters; dressmakers; engravers; film editors; fashion and interior designers; plasterers; structural workers; skincare experts; make-up artists; labourers; models; jewellers and photographers.

Invoke Jophiel for learning new information; especially about spiritual matters; for removing prejudice and ignorance in the world; for preventing abuse by huge organisations and corrupt governments; and for reversing pollution.

Metatron

Day: Sunday

Planet: Pluto

Colour: Maroon, white

Incenses: Carnation, cedar, juniper

Crystals: Sardonyx, mahogany obsidian, flint, peach or red aventurine

Element: Fire

Metal: Gold

The Archangel Metatron is called the Angel of the Lord. In the Kabbalah, the Jewish mystical system, he is placed at the top of the Tree of Life, as the closest Archangel to God's throne.

Originally, Metatron was not an Archangel but the prophet Enoch. After Enoch's death, his body was transformed into flame and surrounded by storms, whirlwinds, thunder and lightning (the latter two being Metatron's attributes). In this way his earthly spirit form was refined into the high Archangel energy vibration.

Because Enoch was a scribe or recorder, Metatron became the heavenly scribe. He lived in the Seventh Heaven, recording all heavenly and earthly events in what are often known as the Akashic records. These records contain not only all experience but also all potential experience and so are important to those who seek to work with the future.

Metatron is chief of all guardian angels. He also teaches children who die young, and in this role is infinitely kind and gentle. He is the tallest of the Archangels and the twin brother of Archangel Sandalaphon.

71

Picture Metatron as an enormous being of brilliant white light with 36 pairs of wings. He carries a pen and a scroll whose contents are hidden from sight.

He is patron of accountants; auditors; writers; civil servants; clerical workers; computer analysts; proofreaders; pilots and drivers; editors and publishers; managers; surveyors; telecommunication workers; teachers of children with learning difficulties or disabilities; foreign correspondents; psychologists and priests.

Invoke Metatron for transformation; upholding family traditions; life reviews and changing life paths; educational ventures, especially bringing education to children in lands where there is little; relieving child poverty and disease; and for long-term research into improving the quality of life and healthcare.

Raziel

Day: Saturday

Planet: Uranus or Neptune

Colour: Dark green

Incenses: Myrrh, poppy, ambergris, any tree incenses (such as cedar)

Crystals: Apache tears, fossils, meteorites, peridots, tektite, any of the aura crystals (such as cobalt, opal, aqua or titanium)

Element: Air

Metal: Lead

Raziel, whose name means 'Secret of God', is the Archangel of divine mysteries and of secrets. He is called Archangel of the Hidden World and is the angel of the unknown and unknowable, because he stands at the veil that separates God from all creation. He is one of the Cherubim.

Raziel is credited with writing the esoteric Book of the Angel Raziel, which contains all earthly and heavenly knowledge. He gave it to Adam as consolation for the loss of Eden, but other angels became jealous and threw it into the sea. God ordered Rahab, angel of the deep caverns of the sea, to restore the book to Adam. Thereafter the book passed to Enoch, then to Noah and finally to King Solomon, who derived from it his magical powers and wisdom. However, it is said that only Raziel can reveal its deepest secrets, to angels and mortals whom he favours.

Raziel is a shadowy Archangel whom you may contact most easily at twilight, on misty days and before dawn, but may not see clearly. Visualise him in grey swirling robes, like an ever-changing grey-green sea. There are deep green flares in his halo. He may also be seen as an outline behind a dark grey, semi-transparent curtain.

Raziel is patron of astrologers and astronomers; clairvoyants; earth and marine scientists; nuclear and radiation workers; Secret Service personnel and all shift workers.

Invoke Raziel for psychic and mystical knowledge; for religious and racial tolerance; to help you access your own deep unconscious wisdom and for the wise use of energy resources in the modern world.

Sandalaphon

Day: Thursday

Planet: Jupiter

Colour: Dark orange

Incenses: Any floral incense

Crystals: Any gems in unpolished form (such as garnet, opal, topaz or sapphire), any calcite or amethyst geode (small crystal inclusions in rock)

Element: Earth

Metal: Tin

Sandalaphon, whose name means 'Brother', is the twin of Metatron. Like Metatron, he was once human. According to the biblical Book of Kings, as the prophet Elijah, he was lifted into heaven by a fiery chariot.

Sandalaphon cares for unborn children and chooses the sex of each of them. He also makes garlands of dreams and memories, and carries the prayers of mortals to God, because he was once human and so understands our concerns.

Visualise Sandalaphon as a very tall angel dressed in shimmering black, like a starry sky filled with comets and shooting stars. He can be identified by his soft, leather openwork shoes, the olive branch he carries, his halo of stars and the small lamb that sometimes accompanies him. He is also sometimes described, like Metatron, as a huge pillar of light.

Sandalaphon is patron of journalists; media workers; midwives; singers and musicians; instrument makers and repairers; family therapists; IVF specialists and nurses; paediatricians; negotiators; obstetricians and gynaecologists.

Invoke Sandalaphon if you are confused about the direction your spiritual path is taking; for all worries concerning fertility, pregnancy, birth and children; for concerns about child neglect and cruelty; for wise guidance to statesmen and world leaders; for inter-generation tolerance; and for acceptance of the differences between nations.

Zadkiel (Sadkiel)

Day: Thursday

Planet: Jupiter

Colour: Sky blue

Incenses: Nutmeg, bergamot, rosemary, ylang ylang

Crystals: Blue celestite, blue howlite, white howlite, blue chalcedony, blue quartz, blue lace agate

Element: Air

Metal: Tin, zinc

Zadkiel's name means 'Righteousness of God'. He is the most gentle of Archangels, good with children and all who are depressed or afraid. He prevented Abraham from sacrificing his son Isaac to God. Zadkiel is also brave. Along with Jophiel, he carries the standard of truth behind Archangel Michael as they march into battle against evil.

Zadkiel is an angel of abundance, spiritual as well as material. He presides over the fair distribution of resources, and as a Throne Archangel stands in the presence of God.

Visualise him with sky-blue wings and surrounded by pale blue light. He carries a ceremonial dagger and a white standard with the white background and red cross of Michael.

Zadkiel is patron of alternative-health practitioners, especially those involved in massage, aromatherapy and other hands-on treatments; actors and actresses; television and radio presenters; mediators; cashiers; prison officers; credit assessors; librarians; interpreters; psychiatrists; and opticians.

Invoke Zadkiel for long-term prosperity; victory; healing those whose minds are troubled; long journeys; increase in abundance; and for major charitable initiatives, especially for the Third World.

Contacting Archangels

Archangel communication is most spiritually uplifting and empowering when we allow the divine presence to guide us. Make quiet time to explore Archangel energies, using the information above, in your angel place once or twice a week, or whenever you feel in need of extra power and protection.

Expect little and remain humble and you may be very pleased with the response. It is when we think we are Gabriel's sole divine reporter on earth that we lose the clarity and simplicity of the communication and switch to ego rather than Archangel mode.

Work with different Archangels and you may find you connect most easily with one or two. Reserve Archangel work for once or twice a month as it is very intense.

A basic ritual for Archangel contact

You can substitute clear quartz or amethyst for any Archangel crystal, and frankincense or sandalwood for any Archangel incense. Pure white or beeswax candles can be used for any Archangel. Keep a pen and paper to hand in case you are moved to write words from the Archangel.

O Choose the Archangel whose wisdom you seek.

O In the evening or early morning – both good Archangel times – light an appropriately coloured candle and an appropriate incense (or fragrance oil if you prefer).

O Hold one of the Archangel crystals or a clear crystal sphere between your hands.

O Welcome the angelic presence and reflect on the qualities of the Archangel and how they are or could be manifested in your life to help others or the planet. If you need to make a petition, do so now – but try not to always contact your chosen Archangel with a request. If you like, you can speak softly aloud, as if to a wise father or mother.

O You may hear a still deep voice like music in your head, or become aware of an aura of holiness in your angel place and perhaps sense the presence of a large, benign, shimmering light form. Or you may just feel a sense of peace. Often, the answers will come in your daily world. Record any special insights in your journal.

Writing a letter to an Archangel

For this ritual, use cream paper and green ink.

O Follow the steps of the basic ritual above.

O When you have welcomed the angelic presence, set your crystal in front of you and begin to write. If you are writing about a personal problem, focus also on the more general aspects. For example, if you are working with Sandalaphon because you are anxious to have a child, also write about concerns for children in your locality or in a particular land who aren't cared for. Perhaps as you write, you can come up with a small way in which to help – for example by giving an hour of your time to teach skills at a local school or youth centre.

O When you are finished, seal the letter in an unmarked envelope and set it beneath the crystal, leaving the incense and candle somewhere where they can to burn through safely (you need not stay during this time). Leave the letter overnight or through the day till sunset if you began at or near dawn.

O Keep the letters, tied with ribbon, in a box – as you did your angel dream letters (see page 49). You do not have to burn them but can store them in a special place when the box is full.

A seven Archangel connection ritual

This is a special ritual for use when you or your family or friends need protection or you want to guard your home against danger. Before you begin, you can name the family members or friends that need protection. You can also use this ritual for sending peace and protection to people, animals or places anywhere in the world. As a bonus, the good wishes you send out will be returned threefold to your personal world.

In this ritual, you will be making the form of a Kabbalistic cross, linking heaven and earth, time and space. We did something similar when we made angel water (see page 55). Kabbalah is a Jewish mystical system from which much of our more general spiritual practice has derived.

If you like you can substitute your own favourite Archangels in the chant.

O Stand in an open place or near the centre of your home, facing north. Raise your power hand (the one you write with) vertically, about three fingers' breadth above you head, and say:

Michael, unto you I raise my spirit.

Picture a pure white sphere of light opening above you like a huge blossoming flower.

O Touch the centre of your brow with your power hand and picture the light flowing down in a shaft of brilliance. Say:

Gabriel, yours is the kingdom and the pathway.

O Touch the centre of your throat and draw the shaft of light further down, saying:

Raphael, be the truth I speak.

O Touch your right shoulder and picture ruby-red light crossing your chest horizontally. Say:

Samael, yours is the power.

O Draw the ruby line across your chest to your left shoulder and see it becoming sky-blue light. Say:

Anael, yours is the love. Enter my heart.

○ Returning to the central line of vertical white light running down the centre of your body, draw down the light, now as golden beams, to your navel, saying:

Sachiel, yours is the glory.

○ Move the line down further, so that it touches your womb or the top of your genitals, now becoming orange. Say:

Cassiel, may your compassion endure for ever and ever.

○ Kneel down and see a shaft of now rose-pink light entering the earth. Say:

Cassiel, Sachiel, Samael, Michael, Anael, Raphael, Gabriel. Archangels all, Amen.

The Archangel wheel

Sometimes we may not be sure which is the best Archangel to work with. The Archangel wheel is a way of divining, using 12 of the main Archangels discussed above. You can change any of the Archangels if you prefer. All you need is a small, flat clear quartz crystal or a small white stone.

Some people like to choose an Archangel from the wheel in the evening before a significant day or event. The result will show which Archangel will protect them during the coming day and also which strengths they will need most. For example, if you are going to be working with confidential material, you might need the tact of Raziel. You can then carry the appropriate Archangel crystal with you and perhaps wear the Archangel's colour to give you extra power.

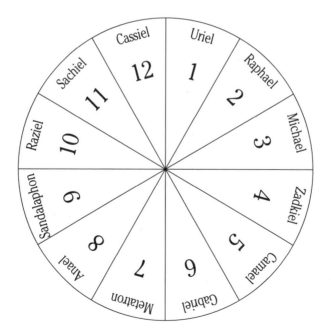

○ You can either use the wheel in the book, or you can photocopy and enlarge it, if you wish adding pictures of the different Archangels (you can download these from the internet or buy them as postcards).

○ Sit close to the wheel and drop the stone or crystal gently on to it. By a process called psychokinesis, your unconscious mind will guide the stone to the right Archangel for your ritual or to give you strength.

○ Look back over this chapter and read the sections on your chosen Archangels, taking note of the qualities they represent and noticing which are relevant to you. You may also find the following key words useful:

1   **Uriel:** transformation, adaptability

2   **Raphael:** widening horizons, healing

3   **Michael:** creativity, inspiration

4   **Zadkiel:** generosity, altruism

5   **Camael:** courage, initiative

6   **Gabriel:** clear communication, intuition

7   **Metatron:** organisation, stamina

8   **Anael:** reconciliation, acceptance

9   **Sandalaphon:** empathy, mediation

10 **Raziel:** confidentiality, tact

11 **Sachiel:** leadership, charity

12 **Cassiel:** compassion, working alone

○ Note if any Archangels appear regularly when you use the wheel, as they may be the ones you need to work with, even if they are not the ones that instantly attract you.

The lists of seven Archangels

The following lists are drawn from traditional angelology and give the names, according to the different traditions, of the seven chief Archangels who stood around the throne of God. The names vary according to the beliefs and priorities of the creators of each list. As you will see from the dates, they are all from very old texts and belief systems. For more detailed information, you might like to consult the classic *Book of Angels* by Gustav Davidson (The Free Press, New York, 1971 – and still in print).

The Book of Enoch and the earliest list

The Book of Enoch was discovered as part of the Dead Sea Scrolls and is not included in the Old Testament. A translation of the original material was published by Oxford Press in 1912 (edited by R H Charles).

1   Uriel

2   Raphael

3   Raguel

4   Michael

5   Zerachiel, Araqael

6   Gabriel

7   Remiel, Jeremiel

The Testament of Solomon list

This is a Greek text from the 2nd century CE, which contains a great deal of information about angels.

1   Mikael

2   Gabriel

3   Uriel

4   Sabrael

5   Arael

6   Iaoth

7   Adonael

The Christian Gnostic list

The Gnostics were breakaway Christian sects who thrived around 150 CE. In addition to the Christian God and his son Jesus Christ, they also believed in a female Goddess of wisdom, Sophia.

1   Michael

2   Gabriel

3   Raphael

4   Uriel, Phanuel

5   Barachiel

6   Sealtiel

7   Jehudiel

The talismanic magic list

This list comes from the Rosicrucian Christian mystical tradition, started in Germany in the early seventeenth century. However, the list may be much older.

1 Zaphkiel

2 Zadkiel

3 Camael

4 Raphael

5 Haniel

6 Michael

7 Gabriel

The hierarchy of blessed angels

This list is from the teachings of the fourth century CE Church father St Augustine of Hippo.

1 Raphael

2 Gabriel

3 Camael

4 Michael

5 Adabiel

6 Haniel

7 Zaphiel

In this chapter we have explored higher sources of angelic wisdom. The Archangels form a core part of any angel work, as they are so very powerful and inspiring. In the next chapter we will be looking at another grouping within the angelic realms, the angels of the natural world.

7

Angels of the Natural World

The angels of the natural world work with the Devas, the shining higher nature essences who make sure the blueprint of nature is followed and fight pollution. Nature angels also care for all the nature essences and spirits, such as elves and dwarves, even those that are bad-tempered. Above all, nature angels strive to keep our planet safe for future generations.

Working with nature angels

The nature angels in this chapter can be invoked in a wide variety of ways. For example, you can carry out regular seasonal rituals with the angels of spring, summer and so on; the angelic protectors of animals can be called upon for the healing of a pet; the angels of seas, rivers, lakes and so on can be invoked for help in combatting water pollution. Include some of the associated symbols, candle colours, crystals and incenses to increase the potency of your working.

A powerful way of bringing the angels' power and protection into your life is to say their names. It doesn't matter if you aren't sure how to pronounce some of them; the pronunciation of most differs from country to country anyway. You can further empower your ritual by including the appropriate Archangel name for the day you are working on (see Chapter 6).

Absorbing the power

Nature angels will fill you with harmony and life force if you allow yourself to welcome the energies of nature into your own energy field. There are many simple ways in which you can do this.

○ Stand in front of a tree, a beautiful pot of flowers, on a lake shore or by the sea. Open your arms wide and high in an arch and slowly breathe in the life force while repeating the names of the nature angels as a soft chant, either in your mind or aloud, on your out-breaths. If you ripple your fingertips in the air, you will feel – and maybe see – the faint haze of the natural aura of the plant or place and become aware of the presence of the angel.

O   Make small, appropriate offerings in places of natural beauty, asking the angels to protect the area. Pick up any litter, especially in urban sites.

O   Take your children, or the children of relatives and friends, regularly to walk or camp in the countryside so that they may learn to respect and value natural beauty and you may absorb some of the revitalising energies of nature. Even children who live in the countryside may spend too much time watching cartoons or playing computer games.

O   Learn about farming and food production, especially organic methods that respect the land.

Angels of the four seasons

Each of the seasons has a presiding angel and helper angels. These angels took over from the seasonal deities of pre-Christian times, and have the same role of ensuring that the wheel of the year continues to turn. They are concerned with the regulation of planting, growth and harvests, and are as relevant if you live in the city as if you live in the countryside. Working with these angels is an important way of connecting with our own inner cycles, even if we have 24/7 heating and lighting. They help us to slow down in the long, cold winter evenings and enjoy the summer nights of light to the maximum.

Each season also has its own angelic crystals, incenses and symbols, which you can put in your angel place to connect with the prevailing energies and opportunities of the season.

Work at the beginning, high point and end of the season. The dates I have given are for the Northern Hemisphere. If you live in the Southern Hemisphere, you should reverse them. Similarly, if you live in a very cold or very hot area, you can adjust the dates I give by up to six weeks so that the actual conditions match the festival energies.

Spring (1 February–30 April)

The central point of this season, when spring energies are at their height, is the spring equinox (21 March), when the days and nights are of equal length.

Archangel: Raphael

Ruling angel: Spugliguel or Milikiel, whose name means 'My Kingdom is God'

Serving angels: Amatiel, Caracasa, Core, Commissoros

Direction: East

Special time of day: Dawn

Colour: Yellow

Incenses: Apple blossom, lavender, fennel, honeysuckle, lemon, violet

Crystals: Citrine, moonstone, opal or angel aura, blue lace agate, angelite

Element: Air

Picture the ruling angels of spring in robes like a brilliant sunrise. The serving angels wear pale green and yellow robes, trimmed with spring flowers. They have pale yellow haloes and wings, the colour of early spring sunshine.

Ask the spring angels to inspire new hopes, new beginnings, new relationships and positive life changes. They can also help with anything to do with fertility, pregnancy, babies, children, newly flowering love, health, moving house and paying the bills you have worried about all winter.

It is well worth making sure you are near a river, lake or coast on Easter Sunday as, if the weather conditions are right and you wake at dawn, you may see the sun dancing in the water and the reflection of the spring angels playing. Your psychic eye will see them even if your physical eye is a little slower.

Symbols to put in your angel place in spring: Spring flowers and newly sprouting greenery; painted or chocolate eggs; seeds planted in pots; feathers; pastel-coloured ribbons and candles; silver coins for the growth of wealth; silver bells hung from plants near an open window to catch the first spring breezes.

Summer (1 May–31 July)

The central point of this season, when summer energies are at their height, is the summer solstice (21 June), when the days are longest.

Archangel: Michael

Ruling angel: Helemmelek or Tubiel

Serving angels: Gargatel, Gaviel, Tariel

Direction: South

Special time of day: Noon

Colour: Gold or orange

Incenses: Chamomile, frankincense, juniper, marigold, orange

Crystals: Amber, carnelian clear quartz crystal, Herkimer diamond, Mexican or crazy lace agate, cobalt aura

Element: Fire

Picture the ruling angels of summer as brilliant gold sunlit forms with glittering wings. The serving angels are dressed in red, orange and gold, and carry baskets of ripening fruit and luxuriant flowers.

Oranir is the chief angel of the summer solstice, or Midsummer's Day. If we speak or sing his name as we celebrate the longest day, we will be protected from all harm.

Ask the summer angels to fill you with confidence, success, happiness, passion, strength and wealth. Ask for their help with issues concerning identity, marriage and partnerships of all kinds. Invoke them to bring to fruition your dreams, to protect adolescents and young adults, and to assist with career advancement and travel plans.

Wake before first light to greet the dawn on the summer solstice. Place some water and all your special angel crystals in a sunny spot to be filled with the light of this most powerful day. You can drink and bathe in the solstice angel water in the days ahead.

Symbols to put in your angel place in summer: Brightly coloured flowers; gold-coloured coins; ripe golden fruit in a clear glass or gold-coloured bowl; orange or gold candles and sun catchers; crystals on cords to hang at windows to reflect rainbows.

Autumn (1 August–31 October)
The central point of this season, when autumn energies are at their height, is the autumn equinox (22 September), when the days and nights are again of equal length.

Archangel: Gabriel

Ruling angel: Torquaret or Melejal

Serving angels: Tahquamn, Guabarel

Direction: West

Special Time of day: Dusk

Colour: Blue or silver

Incenses: Jasmine, myrrh, poppy, rose, rosemary, thyme

Crystals: Aqua aura, blue topaz, green and purple fluorite, strawberry quartz, watermelon or pink tourmaline, rose quartz

Element: Water

Picture the ruling angels in the colours of sunset or brilliant autumn leaves, and the serving angels in softer autumnal colours.

Ask the autumn angels to assist you with all matters of justice and legal affairs, the fruition of long-term goals, reaping the benefits of earlier work and lasting faithful love and relationships. The can help with issues concerning the family, especially adult children, and brothers and sisters. They are concerned with enduring friendships and material security for the months ahead, and will help you to mend quarrels and bring harmony into a frantic life.

Eat nuts or small autumn berries and make wishes for the future, while burying an equal number of seeds or dying leaves to represent what you do not wish to carry forward into the future. Name the autumn Archangel and angels in turn, and ask that they will bless your life.

Symbols to put in your angel place in autumn: Yellow, red or orange leaves – or plants whose leaves are naturally this colour all year; nuts, harvest fruits and berries; knots of corn, wheat or barley; and copper or bronze coins to ensure enough money and happy family relationships.

Winter (1 November–31 January)

The central point of this season, when winter energies are at their height, is the winter solstice (21 December), when the days are at their shortest.

Archangel: Uriel or Raguel

Ruling angel: Attarib or Narel

Serving angels: Amabael, Cetarari

Direction: North

Time of Day: Midnight

Colour: Green, red or white

Incenses: Patchouli, pine, lemon balm, copal, sage, sandalwood

Crystals: Amethyst, aventurine, garnet, heliotrope, hematite, red jasper, ruby, smoky quartz, titanium aura

Element: Earth

Picture the ruling angels of winter in pure white, bearing fiery torches to melt the winter snows. The serving angels have haloes of icicles and shimmering frost wings.

Ask the winter angels to help you with all concerns about property and savings, the home and its furnishings. They preside over older people and animals, and can assist you in overcoming bad luck, healing (especially in the reduction of pain or stress), resting and increasing your spiritual awareness. They are also concerned with letting go of anything destructive, such as addictions, bad influences, obsessions, guilt and fear.

As it gets dark on the shortest day, or the evening before, extinguish all lights except a tiny dark candle on a metal tray. Burn pieces of wool in the dark candle to represent leaving behind the past and then light a tall white or beeswax candle from the dark one to represent the rebirth of light and life. Extinguish the dark candle and dispose of it and the burned wool. Ask for blessings and light from the winter angels.

Symbols to put in your angel place in winter: Fairylights; evergreens, especially holly and pine; a Santa Claus or a small gnome symbol to protect the home; white, green or red candles; frosted-glass snow lanterns with small candles inside; Christmas baubles; small logs of wood shaped into animals or birds.

Angels of natural places

Though we may think of forests, lakes and the seas as under the control of one of the Devas, or higher nature spirits, each natural resource is also protected by angels, who guide the Devas.

If you look back at Chapter 6, you will see that many of the Archangels are involved in nature conservation and the cleansing of pollution. Over the last 30 years, they have become increasingly involved in ecological concerns because of the increased pace of global warming, destruction of tropical rainforests and pollution of the seas. In these areas, angelic help is needed to assist human endeavours.

If you are lucky enough to live in an area of natural beauty, the angels of nature can help to preserve it. Don't take it for granted. But even if you live in the city, the environment is your concern. We are all linked to the wider ecosystem and must all work to counter climate changes caused by greenhouse gas emissions and the melting of the ice caps.

You can connect with the angels of nature anywhere outdoors, be it in a beautiful forest, near a lake or the sea, in a town square, in your own garden or on an apartment balcony. In less lovely places, you can ask the angels to prevent graffiti and unnecessary waste. You can also link to the nature angels through indoor plants, so bringing angelic energies even into your office.

Phul, angel of the lakes, wells and still waters

As well as angel of waters, Phul is also Lord of the Moon, so Monday is his special day. If the moonlight is shining into a lake or a pool, you may see a glimpse of his silvery-blue, almost transparent presence.

Call upon Phul as you stand by a lake, or even a small garden pool, at any time of the day (by moonlight is especially good) or gaze into a silver-coloured bowl filled with water and illuminated by silver candles. Ask him to preserve clear waters on the face of the earth so that all may have clean drinking water and to conserve the water holes and pools of wild animals.

You can also pray to Phul to increase your own intuitive and prophetic wisdom and for all matters concerning women (see also pages 133–6).

Phul also presides over canals and blesses all those who have boats on canals, lakes and inland seas.

Phul's symbols are all water crystals, such as fluorite, calcite and aqua aura;

water plants, willow branches and the wood of all trees that grow near water; freshwater fish, especially small goldfish in a tank; and anything made of silver.

Trsiel, angel of the rivers

Trsiel is the angel of rivers large and small and also estuaries, where the river enters the sea. Picture him in many shades of green, holding a golden oar and with a halo of sparkling rainbow water drops.

Call upon Trsiel if you walk along, fish in or sail flowing rivers. He will regulate the river flow so there is neither drought nor flood. Ask also that new energies and opportunities may flow into your life.

Trsiel's symbols include tiny, wooden model boats; small, perfectly round river stones; glass nuggets or beads in blues and greens, as well as fluorite and aqua aura crystals; flowing indoor water features; and tiny freshwater pearls (you can use beads from an old or broken necklace). Throw dead flowers from a bridge into a river and ask Trsiel to take away sorrow or unhappy memories of the past.

Nahaliel, angel of the running streams

Nahaliel, whose name means 'Valley of God', is the younger brother of Trsiel and presides over smaller bodies of running water. Picture him as much smaller than Trsiel, mistier and in softer greens.

If you have a garden large enough, you could make yourself a tiny stream and waterfall as a focus for Nahaliel. This will have the added benefit of attracting all kinds of water sprites and water creatures into your garden. Nahaliel is a good angel for small children, who can connect with him by having fun playing with water. He also protects children's paddling pools and water parks.

Call upon Nahaliel for the preservation of the all-important small streams that can easily get choked up, filled in or polluted in towns (you can help Nahaliel by unclogging any streams you find on walks). Ask him also for help with small enterprises and ventures, such as starting a one-person business from your home.

His symbols include small, trailing water plants; very tiny, pure white stones and blue and green crystals of any kind; miniature indoor water features (use a fish tank pump) and homemade, indoor water gardens with small wooden stick bridges.

Rahab, angel of the sea

Rahab is a magnificent angel. It was he who retrieved the book of Raziel from the deep (see page 72) and he helped in parting the Red Sea so the Israelites might cross safely. Picture him in deep blues and greens, bearing a trident (like the earlier god Neptune, whom he replaced in Christian lore), striding over the white foaming waves, his white wings billowing like sails.

Occasionally Rahab gets a negative mention in angel lore, because the Church Fathers were very suspicious of powerful forces like the sea. But he is the friend of sailors, ferry operators and all who travel across water. Call on him if you are afraid of travelling by boat and his wings will enfold your ship. He can also be invoked at the times of high tides to protect sea defences in flat lands. On a personal level, he can help if you are suffering as a result of the mood changes or unpredictability of someone in your life, and if you need to recover something that has been lost, whether on land or sea.

His symbols include shells; tiny model mermaids; dried kelp or seaweed (put in a glass jar with whisky it will attract money); small glass fishing floats; aquamarine crystals; pearls; coral and tanks of small saltwater or tropical fish.

Rismuch, angel of agriculture

Rismuch is the angel of all cultivated farm or grazing land. Visualise him swathed in every imaginable shade of brown, carrying a scythe and a hoe as symbols that he is conserver of the land and of the crops.

Call upon Rismuch at the time of sowing and the harvest, even if you live in a city, and whenever you hear that a land is suffering from famine. On a personal level, Rismuch will bring fertility into your life, whether in the form of the birth of a child or the success of a project or business venture.

Rismuch's symbols are sheaves of wheat and ears of corn, dishes of seeds and nuts, and the straw animals or knots tied with red ribbon that are a part of the very ancient folklore of many regions. Light a yellow candle and surround it with these symbols, asking that all may have sufficient food and resources be fairly distributed.

Sofiel, angel of farmers

Sofiel works with Rismuch (see above) and can help farmers everywhere, including those in the Third World who are trying to establish their own agriculture and a system of fairtrade. He also assists Maktiel, angel of fruit and fruit trees (see page 90). Picture him in the rich oranges, reds and yellows of the ripe harvest, with a staff for herding the animals. He especially protects farm horses.

Sofiel is sometimes called the harvest festival angel. Call upon him at the times of the planting and harvest wherever you live, asking that there will be a good harvest – and at any time if you are involved in agriculture. He will also assist you with any restoration project in your life, be it decorating or building a home or improving your finances, even if this will take time to come to fruition.

His symbols include fruits and vegetables that are in season locally; any earth-brown or mottled jaspers and agates; dried corn and wheat knots and animals. In a number of cultures from Scandinavian through eastern and western Europe corn dollies represent the pre-Christian corn mother and later the Virgin Mary. These and fertility animals made of straw are a reminder of the importance of the harvest and the need to invoke blessings from whatever source.

Catharel, angel of gardens and smallholdings

Even if you have only an indoor plant area, Catharel is your angel and will encourage growth and health. He also protects local wildlife gardens and places where native species are cultivated. Picture him with a spade and rake, dressed in soft muted greens and with a pale green halo, so he merges with the garden and can be seen only hazily in bright sunlight. He is most visible on the three days before the full moon, which are good for planting anything that has shoots above ground.

Ask for Catharel's help in creating a beautiful area of plant-life, however small, and in guiding you where and when to plant. You will hear the answer in your mind. Catharel will encourage you towards older, slower, more natural methods of gardening. He will also assist in the recovery of personal health or good fortune.

Catharel's symbols include miniature indoor or special outdoor garden plots dedicated to him; potted plants; trees; moss agate; moonstones and perfectly round; red stones found in the garden or in open spaces.

Sachluph, angel of flowers and herbs

If you love flowers, especially fragrant ones, this is your angel. Dressed in pastel colours and with wings made of thousands of tiny white petals, Sachluph is identifiable by an overwhelming fragrance, especially in the early morning and even near plants that have no scent.

Call upon him for the healthy growth of beautiful flowers and herbs (ask his permission before cutting flowers and herbs) and for healing through natural remedies. He will also restore your sense of beauty and wonder if you are in less than lovely surroundings. Ask his blessing on meals to which you add dried herbs.

His symbols include all fragrant flowers; dried herbs such as lavender, chamomile, rosemary, sage and thyme; herbal pillows and sachets; and small pots of growing herbs.

Zuphlas, angel of the forests and trees

Zuphlas loves huge forestlands and works unstintingly for the conservation of rainforests and for the planting of new forests in industrialised places. He also blesses the revival of ancient forestland, such as the project to recreate Sherwood Forest, home of the legendary Robin Hood, in Nottingham, central England. Picture him in pine-green, carrying a golden axe. He continues the tradition of the pre-Christian forest and nature gods, caring for the wildlife that makes its home in the forest.

Call on him for the preservation of trees, the lungs of the world (one birch tree produces enough oxygen for a family of four) and for your own personal spiritual growth, as well as the physical health and growth of children.

His symbols include anything made of wood, greenery from trees and bushes, pine cones, tree agate, and wild berries and nuts.

Maktiel, angel of fruit and fruit trees

Maktiel preserves all fruit and fruit bushes and trees, from the apple to the more exotic orange, olive and date trees that are now growing in more temperate regions. He encourages the production and consumption of local produce. He is also angel of individual trees. He wears deep green and has wings of mingled orange and pale yellow. He carries an olive branch and a dish of golden apples.

Call on Maktiel for the fertility and growth of fruit and fruit trees throughout the world and for fertility in your own life in every way.

His symbols include bowls of fruit; seeds and pips; miniature indoor trees such as bonsai, palms and small orange trees; ripe berries; and fruit incenses or fragrance oils such as orange, lemon, grapefruit, apple, strawberry and cherry.

Rampel, angel of the hills and mountains

Rampel was present on the first Sabbath after creation. He watches over all who walk or live on or near hills and mountains, endeavouring to prevent landslides and avalanches in winter. Whether you are a hill climber, a skier or simply a lover of high places, he will protect you. He is a very tall and slender angel, whose wings are shrouded in silver mist. He wears deep purple.

Call on Rampel if you or your family members are going hill- or mountain-climbing, if you are afraid of flying (he will enfold the plane), if you live in a hilly region or if you have huge obstacles in your life to overcome.

His symbols include feathers; small ornamental kites; helium balloons; sky crystals such as sodalite, turquoise and lapis lazuli; ferns; wind chimes and mobiles.

Orifiel, angel of the wilderness

Orifiel is the angel for all who love to spend time camping or walking in wild places, as well as those who live in remote areas and desert lands. He presides over the reclamation of land, whether from the sea or from contamination and despoliation. He is sometimes regarded as an Archangel, with dominion over Saturday and the planet Saturn, so this is a good day to contact him.

Visualise Orifiel as ever-changing, sometimes like mountain peaks at sunset, sometimes like deep dark forests, sometimes like deep blue lakes, but always with wings like rainbows. Call on him before a camping trip or if a friend or relative is going backpacking abroad. He will protect adult family members far from home and will help you if you feel lost or alone in your life.

His symbols include tiny compasses, maps or pictures of your favourite wild places; turquoise or sodalite crystals; souvenirs of your travels made of natural materials; old and future travel tickets, and photographs of absent family members.

Angels of animals and wildlife

There are a number of nature angels who care for animals and birds. You might like to offer your prayers to them for the health of your own pets, for the survival of endangered species and for the welfare of creatures who are cruelly treated. They will send comfort and healing to animals that are are sick or very young or old, and will help pets to find their way home if they stray.

Remember to help the wildlife angels by feeding wild birds and working to preserve natural habitats in gardens, especially in cities. In every country, indigenous species are threatened with extinction because of modern high-tech farming methods and global warming.

Teach children about animals and birds, especially local wildlife. Some modern children are more familiar with characters in computer games than with common wildlife species such as blackbirds. Take children to wildlife conservation areas, especially those where less exotic but equally precious local wildlife is conserved. Take wildlife photographs to post on the internet or to send to local schools and daycare centres.

As a reward for your efforts, blessings will come into your life in small but exciting ways, such as seeing a beautiful rare bird quite motionless outside your window or a fabulously coloured butterfly settling on flowers in front of your children.

Manakiel (Manakel): angel of aquatic animals and fish

Manakiel protects dolphins, whales, seals and all tropical and coldwater fish.

Picture him in green-blue robes, carrying a huge seashell, in which he can hear the call of any distressed sea creatures.

His healing crystals are aquamarine or blue coral, which you can set in fish tanks.

The Archangel Azrael (see page 69) is also associated with fish and protects fishermen at sea.

Anpiel, angel of birds

Anpiel protects all smaller birds, whether wild or tame, and lives in the seventh heaven.

Picture him in a brown and grey cloak of feathers, carrying a basket filled with grain, with which he feeds the birds in winter.

His healing crystals are lapis lazuli, sodalite and (for tiny birds) blue lace agate. You can place his crystals in birdcages and aviaries for protection or bury one beneath a bird table.

(Tubiel, one of the angels of summer, will help to return lost small birds to their owners.)

Alfun, angel of doves

Alfun is the angel of doves.

He is dressed in silvery grey.

His healing crystals are moonstone, blue lace agate and angelite. If you have doves or pigeons, place one of these crystals in the dovecote or pigeon loft. If you have a bird-table set one of them near it to attract doves to your garden.

Trgiaob, angel of wild and water fowl

Trgiaob protects wild fowl such as wild ducks, geese, swans and pheasants. He also guards wild snakes and all insects, from spiders to moths and butterflies and the essential worker bees.

Picture Trgiaob in a magnificent feather cloak, his wings sprouting feathers of all the creatures he protects.

His healing crystals are green and brown jasper. Hold one of these to send his protection to wild birds as they begin migration or when lakes are frozen. Also keep one of Trgiaob's crystals near beehives.

Hariel, angel of domesticated animals

Hariel protects and heals all our pets, as well as horses that we use for riding or to pull carts and wagons. He is one of the Cherubim and also rules science, especially where it helps with animal welfare.

Picture Hariel as a sturdy brown and yellow angel, surrounded by all kinds of pets.

His healing crystals are Dalmatian jasper, cat's eye, snowflake obsidian (best for horses) and rutilated quartz.

If your pet is ill, choose two crystals of any of the kinds listed above (either two different ones or two the same). Take one in each hand and circle them clockwise, close to the animal, up and down the body, asking that the healing power of Hariel restore your pet to health. It is a good idea to perform this ritual monthly, asking Hariel to keep your pet healthy.

If you have a more exotic pets, such as a lizard or snake, place mookaite or one of the mottled jaspers in its tank.

Behemiel, angel of tame animals

Behemial is the protector of farm animals, goats, poultry and all working animals, such as guide dogs and guard dogs. He ensures that animals have fresh water and warm bedding, especially in winter. He is sometimes twinned with Hariel.

Another high-ranking angel, Behemial is dressed in browns and yellows, and carries straw and a pitcher of water.

Behemial's crystals include flint, brown patterned agates, dark-green jade, and fossils, any of which you can keep in animal stalls. If you work with farm animals, ask the blessing of Behemiel as you set a crystal in each pen at the beginning of winter. Wash the crystals at the beginning of spring and leave them outdoors for a few hours before replacing them, with thanks to Behemiel for his care.

Hayyel, angel of wild animals

As the angel of wild animals, whether living in the wild or in conservation parks, Hayyel is primarily a conservation angel. He presides over wise hunting for food and the compassionate hunter. He protects endangered species, and fiercely guards wild animals that are badly kept or exploited.

Picture Hayyel in green, carrying a horn and a bow and arrow.

His crystals are carnelian, red agate and tiger's eye. Place one of these on or near any pictures in the newspaper of threatened wildlife or reports of poachers, asking Hayyel to cast his circle of light and protection around the creatures.

The Archangel Uriel also guards endangered species.

Afriel, angel of young animals

A gentle but fiercely protective angel, Afriel represents young animals and pregnant or nursing mothers of any species. He will assist from the moment an animal is pregnant to the time the young must leave the mother. He also guards rescue centres and abandoned animals.

Picture Afriel surrounded by green and blue mists. He bears a huge silver sword to drive away all harm from the young and from nursing mothers.

His healing crystals are blue chalcedony or angelite, and pink rose quartz or calcite. Visualise a circle of pink light around any animal in labour and ask Afriel to assist her. Send a small Afriel crystal with each of the young to their new homes and leave one with the mother for comfort for at least nine days after the separation. Place one of Afriel's crystals under the bed of any newly acquired rescue animal – it will help them to settle.

Angels of the weather

Angels preside over the weather. We can invoke them for better weather conditions or use the energies of the weather to endow ourselves with particular angelic strengths. A word of warning: when you are working with the weather, always ask that the conditions you are invoking do not cause harm to anyone or disrupt the natural cycles in any way.

Diane, who lives in Somerset, England, gave me the following account in 1995:

I was crippled with an illness and unable to walk. I had a daughter of three. It had been raining hard all morning, but I was not at all anxious. At about two o'clock in the afternoon, I suddenly heard a male voice I did not recognise urging me again and again: 'Get your child. Leave everything and get out of the house.'

At first I thought it was my imagination, but the voice became more and more insistent. At last I phoned for a taxi to take us to my sister's house. That evening a local river burst its banks and the downstairs of my house was flooded by several feet of water. Had I stayed, I would have been trapped there with my daughter.

I am convinced that Diane's saviour was either her guardian angel or an angel of the rains.

Even in the modern technological world, we cannot fail to be aware of the weather – as we dig the car out after an early snowfall, water a parched garden or worry about rising river levels. In some places the weather can cause catastrophes, in the form of floods, droughts, whirlwinds and violent storms. Whether we are personally affected by these ravages of weather or have simply seen them on the television news, we can call on the angels of the weather for help – and then do whatever we can, however small, to enable practical relief, perhaps by sending money, volunteering with an aid agency or raising awareness.

It is important that we keep in touch with the weather and encourage our children to take pleasure in different climatic conditions – flying kites in the wind, throwing snowballs and making snowmen and snowhouses in the snow, splashing in the puddles on a rainy day. If you are feeling jaded or unenthusiastic, experience the extremes of your local climate and fill yourself with the life force as you play again like a child.

The following are the most commonly recognised angels of the weather. Because the weather is such a powerful and often unpredictable force, it has more than its share of Archangels.

Michael, Archangel of weather

Michael is Lord of all the weather angels. He oversees winds, storms, snow and the rain necessary for the crops. Call upon Michael to guard crops and homes against adverse weather conditions and to relieve drought. Call upon him also to bring the sun back into your life after sorrow.

For more information about Michael see page 62.

Gabriel, Archangel of inclement weather

Gabriel is protector against all inclement weather, especially that encountered while travelling. Invoke him before any long journey.

For more information about Gabriel see page 61.

Metatron, Archangel of extreme weather

You will probably recall that Metatron was surrounded by storms, whirlwinds, thunder and lightning when he was transformed from the prophet Enoch into an Archangel (see page 71).

Metatron is another angel of protection against unusual or adverse weather conditions. Invoke him also if you need to take a stand against bullies.

Raguel (Raquil/Rufael), Archangel of ice and snow

Candle colour: Deep blue

Incense: Ginger, cinnamon

Crystal: Snow or milky quartz

Raguel is an Archangel we haven't met before. His name means 'Friend of God', and, as well as presiding over ice and snow, he ensures the good conduct of the other angels by his own example. He is an Archangel of the Earth, who is said to bring forth the other angels of ice and snow at the last Judgement.

Visualise him in dark grey and silver robes, with a halo glittering with icicles. His fiery sword, like that of Uriel, melts the winter snows.

Call upon him in the coldest winter to bring relief, perhaps on a day when you need to drive a long distance. Call on him when you need to melt prejudice and opposition in your life.

Raphael, Archangel of the wind

In the days of sailing ships, Raphael was invoked by sailors to prevent their ships becoming becalmed. Call on him also if you need to overcome stagnation in your life or any fears about safety while travelling.

For more information about Raphael see page 63.

Remiel, Archangel of storms

Candle colour: Dark red

Incense: Sandalwood, copal

Crystal: Garnet, red tiger's eye

Remiel, another Archangel we haven't yet encountered, is Lord of Thunder and Storms. He stands in God's presence, and his name means 'He whom God raises up'.

Picture Remiel in a chariot of gold riding through the stormy skies.

Call on Remiel for protection from storms and storm damage and also when you feel helpless and need to bring power into your life.

Barkiel, angel of the storm

Candle colour: Indigo

Incense: Pine

Crystal: Hematite, iron pyrites

Barkiel is also angel of lightning and hail, as well as ruler over February.

Visualise him in dark robes, with dark wings that blaze momentarily as lightning flashes shoot from his halo.

Invoke Barkiel for protection against storm damage, lightning strikes and thunderbolts. Call on him also for energy when you are exhausted and for protection against envy.

Galgaliel, angel of the sun

Candle colour: Gold

Incense: Frankincense, orange

Crystal: Clear quartz crystal, Herkimer diamond

Galgaliel is the Lord of the Sun and of the sun wheel as it turns though the year. He presides over sunshine, especially in the middle of the day.

He has a golden halo and golden robes, and carries a wheel of gold. His wings are made of pure sunlight.

Call on Galgaliel for sunshine to ripen the crops, and also when you need the sun for a special outdoor celebration. Call upon him also to bring joy on grey days. He is a wonderful antidote to Seasonal Affective Disorder (caused by lack of sunlight). Fill a crystal bowl with water and try to capture sunlight in it. If this is impossible, use golden candles to draw down the sunshine, as you call Galgaliel's name nine times.

Iris, angel of the rainbow

Candle colour: Two- or three-coloured, pink

Incense: Jasmine, lavender, rose

Crystal: Rainbow quartz, rainbow obsidian, cobalt aura.

Iris is an Ancient Greek female angel. She reminds us that the rainbow is a sign of God's forgiveness and a promise of happier times ahead. She also comforts bereaved husbands, who traditionally plant an iris on their wife's grave, and sorrowing sons and daughters who have lost a mother.

Iris has rainbow wings and carries a beautifully formed purple and yellow iris and a golden lily.

Call on Iris when you see a rainbow and remember that life is of worth and things will get better. Call on her also for reconciliation with estranged family and for surviving loss of all kinds. (For more information on Iris, see pages 10 and 134.)

Mathariel, Ridya and Zalbesael, angels of the rain

Candle colour: Grey

Incense: Lemon, thyme

Crystal: Jade, green jasper, called the rain stone

These angels can, traditionally, both bring rain and prevent the extremes of excessive flooding or drought.

Visualise them in constantly moving robes of grey and blue, with dark grey wings that shed raindrops.

If you need to bring rain, chant their names continuously nine times, starting with Mathariel, while scattering circles of water drops over a bowl of dry soil or sand. If you need to stop the rain, chant the names continuously nine times in reverse order, while lighting a grey candle over a bowl of water. Leave the candle to burn through in a safe place.

Moriel, Ruhiel, Rujiel and Ben Nez, the angels of the four winds

Colour: Silver

Incense: Lemon, lemongrass

Crystal: Tektite, blue lace agate, smoky quartz, apache tears (use one of the crystals or a mixture of all four)

The angels of the four winds live in high places. They are the servants of Metatron (see pages 71 and 94) and can most easily be contacted on hilltops and open treeless plains.

Picture them as formed from clouds, with constantly moving shapes that appear and disappear from view, only to reappear instantly.

Call on the four angels in turn three times in order to bring wind – whether to move a sailboat or dry your washing – or to bring change into your life. Reverse the order of the names and chant them three times more to diminish the winds.

Su'iel, angel of earthquakes

Candle colours: Mustard-yellow, cream

Incense: Any spice fragrance

Crystal: Mookaite

Su'iel is invoked in earthquake zones to protect against earth tremors and damage caused by them.

Picture him in sandy yellows and clay-red, bearing a huge staff with a serpent head, with which he strikes the earth.

Call on Su'iel if you live in an earthquake area or if you hear of a natural disaster in another part of the world. Call upon him also to guard against unwelcome disruption in your life.

Zaamiel, angel of tempestuous winds

Candle colour: Dark grey

Incense: Fennel, lavender

Crystal: Lepidolite, sugilite.

Zaamiel is the angel of hurricanes, whirlwinds, tornadoes and so on. He protects homes in places where such winds are frequent. However, because hurricanes affect the weather systems thousands of miles away, he is also an important angel for bringing calm weather in other lands, especially when a hurricane is reported as imminent somewhere in the world.

Zaamiel is surrounded by swirling clouds. He wears windswept, silver-grey robes and has billowing wings.

Call on Zaamiel for protection against high winds and gales that may damage property. Call on him also for a period of calm if you have a troubled home life or temperamental family members.

Cloud angels

Angels often appear in cloud formations. These cloud angels are most often seen at sunset, but sometimes at other times of the day. Angelic cloud pictures are different in quality and intensity from other cloud images and manifest as complete formations with distinctive angel wings and faces. Angel sky images may be perceived at a time of acute stress or need in the life of the perceiver and answer a question or herald a positive change.

Cloud angels cannot be explained away purely as meteorological phenomena because of their clarity and and the way they fade quite suddenly and dramatically. They may be seen by a number of people at the same time and may be accompanied by a spinning sun or the flooding of the sky with momentary brilliance.

In Exodus 20–22 it is recorded that the Angel of the Lord travelled through the desert ahead of and all around the Israelites in a pillar of cloud. The angel was seen as a dark cloud during the day, when the sun was bright, and as a flame at night in the darkness.

The Hill of the Angels is above Nevern, near Tenby, in south-west Wales. It is close to the sacred megalithic dolmen of Pentre Ifan, which was used by Druids for initiation ceremonies. St Brynach, an Irish-born Celtic monk, used regularly to climb the hill to talk to the angels who appeared in cloud formation above it at sunrise and sunset. You can see the angels today on the hilltop when the weather is clear.

Even more intriguing are reports – denied by official sources at the time – that in 1990 Russian cosmonauts saw an angelic form outside the window of their spacecraft during a flight. It had golden wings. As a result, the astronauts were brought home early.

But most angel-cloud sightings are by ordinary people and occur only once. Heidi, who lives in Bruges, Belgium, told me her story when I was enjoying a short break there in January 2004. We met in the magnificently painted Church of the Holy Blood, where we were both admiring the jewel-coloured angels on the walls. Heidi told me how a few months earlier she had been desperately worried about her 18-year-old son Johannes, who had not contacted her for several weeks since walking out of the home after a quarrel with her new partner.

One evening, before dusk, Heidi was sitting alone on a bench, looking out over the water meadows near the Beguines Abbey on the outskirts of Bruges. The Beguines were medieval women who were not nuns but chose to live, often with their children, in a spiritual community. Heidi says:

> *On the clear, flat, frosty horizon, I saw a huge silver and gold angel who seemed to fill the sky. No-one else was around. In that moment I knew my son was safe. The next morning he telephoned asking to meet me.*

Heidi told me she had realised in the intervening months that her new partner was very controlling and they had separated. Johannes had not returned home but was living in nearby Antwerp, and mother and son now have a warm relationship again. Johannes said that in the early evening, the day before he phoned, the sunset had been flooding into his apartment and he was filled with love and knew he had to call his mother.

Nature angels do help us to work with nature at its most beautiful and ideal, so that we can, through earthly natural places, tap into the most beautiful forest imaginable. They can also help to reverse the modern trends of pollution and despoiling the environment. In the next section we will look at angels and how they affect our destiny.

8

Angels and
Your Date of Birth

In this chapter, we will be looking at angels linked with your birth, who – like your guardian angel – can guard and guide you. There are many possibilities for choosing angelic support based on the calendar. The ones we will be looking at here are:

○ Birthday angels (who each rule a group of five days)

○ Angels of the zodiac (who each rule a zodiac sign)

○ Angels of the month (who each rule a calendar month)

Birthday angels

We all have a special birth angel who oversees our life path and who rules the day we were born. Each birth angel rules over five days.

Our birth angel can be invoked on birthdays, at marriages and at the birth of our own children, when our birth angel joins the child's birth angel to ease the labour and delivery. At a marriage, the birthday angels of the couple unite to make the occasion a happy day and the union joyous.

You might be wondering how a single angel can be at everyone's birthday celebration at the same time. Angels are not separate individuals contained within a single body as humans are, though we think of them and relate to them most easily that way. Angels are made of pure energy and so can be in different places at the same time. Their energies are so vast and diffuse (hard to imagine) that we can all call upon our birth angel whenever we need them. For our birthday angel is special and will protect us every day of the year.

Visualise your birthday angel in your own way. Ask him or her to appear to you in a dream on your birthday or to let you see an image of him or her in your mind.

Since birthday angels are linked with zodiac angels, you can use the zodiacal colours, crystals and fragrances listed below to talk to your birth angel at any time, and on your birthday or wedding day.

All this can also work the other way around. If you need to set a date for a specific occasion, be it a special holiday, a celebration or a business meeting, you can choose it by looking for a five-day angel whose energies are right for the event and then going for a date within this angel's rulership. For example, 6–10 May are good dates for a difficult family get-together with troublesome relatives, since they are governed by the angel Aladiah, who brings stability to unstable situations and calms excessive emotions. Because these dates fall within Taurus, you would be able to light pink candles, put rose quartz crystals round your home and burn rose and apple blossom incenses or fragrance oils to add further calm (these being the candle colours, crystals and incenses associated with Taurus). If you are born on 29 February you have two angels.

The birthday angels are as follows:

21–25 March: Vehuiah: One of the Seraphim, who answers prayers and rules the morning rays of the sun at the spring equinox, so offering a new start and the resolution of old problems.

26–30 March: Jeliel: Another Seraph, who once ruled over those lands where Europe merges with Asia. He ensures that rulers and high officials act justly and assists all who are unfairly treated or oppressed. In addition, he is the angel of faithful married love and so is a good angel at weddings at any time.

31 March–4 April: Sitael: An angel who helps in times of hardship. He rules those who are born in fortunate material circumstances or who gain wealth, encouraging them to use their advantages to help others.

5–9 April: Elemiah: Another Seraph, he protects those who travel, especially by sea. He also protects against road rage and traffic accidents.

10–14 April: Mahasiah: An angel of mysteries who bears one of the secret names of God and can reveal answers to secrets that are worrying you. He helps you to keep confidences and brings unexpected gifts of all kinds.

15–20 April: Lelahel: Rules over love, both family and romantic, art in all forms, science and technology. He also brings good luck.

21–25 April: Achaiah: Another of the Seraphim, he knows the secrets of nature and will reveal them to those who listen in quiet beautiful places. He is also the angel of patience and those who show this virtue.

26–30 April: Catharel (Cahetel): Also angel of gardens and smallholdings (see page 89), he is invoked to improve the growth of agricultural crops and so is an angel of abundance and fertility in all its forms.

1–5 May: Haziel: One of the Cherubim, he shows compassion to all who feel abandoned and lonely. He brings light into the darkness, whether physical (dark nights) or emotional (despair).

6–10 May: Aladiah: Brings stability to unstable situations and calms excessive emotions, ensuring that critical words are softened and negativity is reduced.

11–15 May: Lauviah: Angel of those who are naturally talented and feel different because of their knowledge or gifts. He helps them to value and develop their unique potential and world-view.

16–20 May: Hahaiah: Another Cherub, he helps to preserve traditions, especially traditional crafts, and reveals hidden mysteries of lost worlds and wisdom to mortals.

21–25 May: Iehalel: Has dominion over justice and acts as advocate of those who are unjustly accused and abused by prejudice or repressive systems of belief.

26–31 May: Mebahel: A kind of Robin Hood angel who redistributes wealth and defends those whose income is threatened through unemployment, natural disasters or disability.

1–5 June: Hariel: Protects pets, horses and all tame creatures (see also page 92). He rules science and is a patron of the arts. He can also be invoked against spite and malice, and cruelty to animals.

6–10 June: Hakamiah: One of the Cherubim and guardian of France. He will guard us against treachery and false friends. He also guards against unwise investments and contracts.

11–15 June: Lauviah: Encourages all who seek to communicate their gifts, whether through writing, inventions or technological skills. (Not to be confused with Lauviah the angel of Taurus and 11–15 May, who has the same name but is a different angel.)

16–21 June: Caliel: An angel from the choir of Thrones who will swiftly aid all who are in trouble in perilous places or situations or live in communities where security is a problem.

22–26 June: Leuviah: Another angel of the mysteries who helps us to avoid unwarranted intrusion in our lives, as well as those who would steal credit for our ideas (and in the modern world, identify fraud).

27 June–1 July: Pahaliah: Helps to spread faith among the sceptical and teaches spirituality in diverse forms. He also encourages high standards of conduct.

2–6 July: Nelchael: An angel of the Thrones who teaches astronomy, mathematics and knowledge of the world's lands and climate. He encourages ecological awareness and responsibility.

7–11 July: Yeiayel: Protects and brings loving warmth to the home and family and ensures that absent members and the wider family circle keep in touch.

12–16 July: Mehalel: Another mystical angel who draws a veil over past losses and betrayal, and uplifts us with promises of a better tomorrow.

17–22 July: Hahueuiah: His name means 'Service to others and respect for traditional values'. He encourages the young to respect and value older family members.

23–27 July: Nithaiah: The angel of poets, from the choir of Dominions. He is an angel of prophecy and protects peacemakers and all who spread peace through their words, whether written or spoken.

28 July–1 August: Haaiah: Another Dominions angel, whose special role is overseeing diplomacy and negotiations between nations. He seeks to soften the hearts of dictators and to reduce war-mongering and the panic that can lead to war.

2–6 August: Yeratel: Another Dominions angel, he is a light-bringer and a defender of liberty and human rights, protecting those imprisoned unfairly, especially far from home.

7–12 August: Seheiah: Protects against disease and illness, and also against disasters small and large caused by fire, earthquake, whirlwind or flood.

13–17 August: Reiiel: An angel of Dominions, he encourages idealism among leaders and altruism towards poorer nations. He also works towards the fair election of leaders everywhere.

18–22 August: Omael: Brings fertility and increase to all the species on the earth and encourages diversity of languages and cultures. He also assists chemists and pharmacists.

23–28 August: Lecabel: Rules over vegetation, the fertility of the land and the growth of the crops. He is a patron of agricultural workers and those in the food processing industries, and works to ensure that food is kept natural and pure.

29 August–2 September: Vasairiah: A ruling angel of justice, the legal system and all who administer justice in courts. He promotes environmental, domestic and civil rights.

3–7 September: Yehudiah: A kindly angel who brings hosts of gentle angels to relieve the dying and gently carry their souls to the afterlife. He also comforts the bereaved.

8–12 September: Lehahiah: From the angelic order of Powers, he protects orderly democracies and encourages the balance between fair and representative government and civil obedience to wise laws.

13–17 September: Chavaquiah: Another angel of mysteries, he encourages quietness, stillness and contemplation, and so is a good angel to work with in the modern frantic world.

18–23 September: Menadel: An angel of the order of Powers, he blesses all who are far from their native land, whether in exile or for work or financial reasons.

24–28 September: Anael: An Archangel (see page 67), he guards the gates of the West Wind and so brings gentle rain. He also brings comfort to older people and those of any age who are disabled.

29 September–3 October: Haamiah: An angel of the Powers, he encourages the peaceful co-existence of different faiths and religious tolerance. He is also an angel of integrity and honesty.

4–8 October: Rehael: An angel of the choir of Powers, he brings good health and long life and also helps parents in their task of helping their offspring to become kind and follow the paths that are right for them.

9–13 October: Ihiazel: Angel of negotiations and negotiators and all attempts at mediating, whether between individuals, family factions, colleagues, groups or nations.

14–18 October: Hahahel (Hahael): From the angelic choir of Virtues, he watches over aid- and charity-workers and missionaries at home and abroad.

19–23 October: Mikael: Banishes corruption in official bodies, organisations and companies, and helps all in positions of authority to be just and impartial.

24–28 October: Veuliah: From the choir of Principalities, he assists in making life-changes and in softening stubborn destructive attitudes in others.

29 October–2 November: Yelaiah (Elaiah): Angel of inspiration and illumination, and of starlight. He promises the fulfilment of realistic dreams.

3–7 November: Sahaliah: One of the choir of Virtues, he rules fruit and vegetables and their harvest. As well as the natural production of fruit and vegetables, he encourages humane farming methods.

8–12 November: Ariel: One of the great Prince angels, he is sometimes said to rule the waters and the winds and is called the Lord of the Earth. Ariel is a healer, especially of animals and birds. In his role as a birth angel he brings the transformation of sickness into health and exhaustion into energy – for humans and animals alike, as well as for the planet. He encourages kindness towards all creatures. (See also page 68.)

13–17 November: Asaliah: From the order of Virtues, he is powerful in righting injustice while at the same time diminishing the desire for vengeance or retribution. Thus he is good in times of riot or civil or ethnic disturbance and in healing acrimonious divorce or inheritance disputes.

18–22 November: Mihael: Comes from the angelic choir of Virtues and is the angel of married love and fidelity. He also blesses the birth of children and protects the mother while in labour and during the weeks after giving birth.

23–27 November: Vehuel: An angel of the Principalities, he encourages original creative thinking and the teaching of new ideas, both in writing and verbally, to stimulate the minds of the young.

28 November–2 December: Daniel: an angel of the choir of Principalities, he is concerned with those who administer and practise the law, also accountants and taxation officials, seeking to ensure that they exercise the highest standards of honesty and fairness.

3–7 December: Hahaziah: Another angel of mysteries, he seeks to expand human consciousness and the spiritual potential of individuals. He also brings a more spiritual focus to family life and society generally.

8–12 December: Imamiah: A Principalities angel who assists all who travel, especially long distance, such as truck drivers and those who drive many miles to and from work each day. In the modern world, he is a powerfully protective angel against threats of terrorism.

13–16 December: Nanael: Another Principalities angel, he rules over scholarship, science, philosophy and religion. He helps students with learning difficulties, whether caused by social, emotional, physical or intellectual problems.

17–21 December: Nithael: Also of the Principalities, he rules over international bodies such as NATO and the United Nations where issues such as peace, famine relief and environmental responsibility are concerned. He also oversees international aid workers, charity organisers and fundraisers.

22–26 December: Mebahiah: An angel of fertility, he helps those who want children but are having difficulties conceiving. He is also an angel of conscience, encouraging humans to be their own regulators of honourable conduct.

27–31 December: Poiel: A Principalities angel, he is guardian of the future we have yet to make. He is active in assisting us to make wise choices about that future.

1–5 January: Nemamiah: Stands at the gates of the New Year and protects all who are poor or afraid about the future. He guards especially the very old, children and animals, and any who are too weak to ask for their rights.

6–10 January: Ieilael: Another angel of the future, encouraging caution and preparation, so that the foundations of security and stability are laid and finances are conserved.

11–15 January: Harael: Called the Shining One, he is patron of all schools, libraries, colleges, universities, archives and museums, and blesses all who study or work in them. He also encourages the use of traditional knowledge to make discoveries about the past.

16–20 January: Mitzrael: Encourages the spread of freedom of speech, action and equality for women and oppressed minorities in less liberal societies.

21–25 January: Umabel: Rules over the physical sciences and laboratories, astronomy and observatories and space exploration. Safety and integrity of purpose are his watchwords, both for individuals and globally.

26–30 January: Iahhel: An angel of pure light who watches over all who walk a solitary or lonely path, whether working or living alone, and also those who seek inner stillness through meditation and contemplation.

31 January–4 February: Anauel: Protects all who work in commercial, property and financial organisation, including bankers and brokers. He is concerned especially with the stability of financial markets so that poorer individuals and societies will not suffer from sudden losses. Above all, he campaigns for a good standard of living for everyone.

5–9 February: Mehiel: Angel of writers and poets, public speakers, researchers and lecturers, especially new or struggling ones. He encourages free speech in plays and books worldwide, but at the same time supports wise censorship of what might corrupt the young (in the modern world this includes computer games).

10–14 February: Damabiah: Oversees shipbuilding and naval vessels, and in the modern world the safe construction and flight of aircraft, as well as safety at ferryports and airports.

15–19 February: Manakiel: The protector of all sea creatures, from dolphins to fish, he is also increasingly concerned with clean seas and the preservation of fish stocks through wise fishing. (See also page 91).

20–24 February: Eiael: Angel of the mystical arts, spiritual studies, alternative health and alternative spirituality, also of long life and good health.

25–28 February: Habuiah: Another angel of abundance and the fertility of the land, crops and animals, as well as people. He is a reminder that we are all linked through the cycles of the seasons.

1–5 March: Rochel: Finds lost people, animals and birds, and can be invoked for the return of lost or stolen property.

6–10 March: Gabamiah: Angel of sacred chanting, song and music. He blesses all who perform, write or take pleasure in musical arts, whether for pleasure or professionally.

11–15 March: Haiaiel: Angel of painters, calligraphers, etchers and all who create beautiful things with their hands and imagination. He encourages teaching skills to new generations.

16–20 March: Mumiah: Angel of medicine and all doctors, nurses and medical practitioners, as well as wise alternative and spiritual healers. He is also invoked to bring miracles in hopeless cases.

Angels of the Zodiac

A different angel oversees each of the zodiac sun signs. So why is a zodiac angel necessary when you have a birthday angel and a month angel? The answer is that we can't get too much help!

Your zodiac angel is like the big brother of your birthday angel. You can ask for his help not only on your birthday but also at any time in your life when you need his extra strength.

Remember, too, that whatever conventional zodiacal sources tell you about the compatibility of a future partner, it is important to look at the angelic associations. You may find that, contrary to what the stars tell you, your angel will get on rather well with your potential partner's angel, which means that the match is well augured.

♈ Aries

Symbol: The ram

Dates: 21 March–20 April

Ruling angel: Machidiel (or Malahidael)

Strengths: Self-confidence, strong identity, innovation, assertiveness, action

Colour: Red

Crystals: Carnelian, diamond, Herkimer diamond

Incenses: Cedar, dragon's blood

Planet: Mars

Element: Fire

♉ Taurus

Symbol: The bull

Dates: 21 April–21 May

Ruling angel: Asmodel

Strengths: Persistence, patience, reliability, loyalty, practical abilities, stability, love of beauty

Colour: Pink

Crystals: Rose quartz, emerald

Incenses: Rose, apple blossom

Planet: Venus

Element: Earth

♊ Gemini

Symbol: The heavenly twins

Dates: 22 May–21 June

Ruling angel: Ambriel (Ambiel)

Strengths: Excellent communication skills, adaptability, scientific/technological aptitude, curiosity, intelligence, versatility

Colours: Pale yellow, grey

Crystals: Citrine, sapphire

Incenses: Lavender, lemongrass

Planet: Mercury

Element: Air

♋ Cancer

Symbol: The crab

Dates: 22 June–22 July

Ruling angel: Muriel

Strengths: Sensitivity, kindness, imagination, homemaking, nurturing (especially of children), creating emotional security, keeping secrets

Colour: Silver

Crystals: Moonstone, pearl

Incenses: Lemon balm, jasmine

Planet: Moon

Element: Water

♌ Leo

Symbol: The lion

Dates: 23 July–23 August

Ruling angel: Verchiel (Zerachiel)

Strengths: Power, courage, generosity, nobility, idealism, leadership, protection of the weak, ability to perform creatively in public

Colour: Gold

Crystals: Clear crystal quartz, golden topaz

Incenses: Frankincense, orange

Planet: Sun

Element: Fire

♍ Virgo

Symbol: The maiden

Dates: 24 August–22 September

Ruling angel: Hamaliel

Strengths: Striving for perfection, organisational skills and methodical attention to detail, efficiency, healing powers, ability to persevere with a routine but necessary task though to the end, reliability

Colour: Green

Crystals: Jade, opal

Incenses: Patchouli, thyme

Planet: Mercury

Element: Earth

♎ Libra

Symbol: The scales

Dates: 23 September–23 October

Ruling angel: Zuriel

Strengths: Harmony, ability to see both sides of a question and to incorporate different viewpoints, diplomacy, peace-making skills, a strong sense of justice, charisma (especially with the opposite sex)

Colour: Light blue

Crystals: Lapis lazuli, blue topaz

Incense: Lemon verbena, vanilla

Planet: Venus

Element: Air

♏ Scorpio

Symbol: The scorpion

Dates: 24 October–22 November

Ruling angel: Bariel (Baruel)

Strengths: Intensity, spiritual and psychic awareness, ability to transform self and a situation, the power to start over again or revive an unpromising or stagnant situation

Colour: Burgundy

Crystals: Aquamarine, aqua aura

Incenses: Pine, mint

Planet: Pluto

Element: Water

♐ Sagittarius

Symbol: The archer

Ruling angel: Adnachiel (Advachiel)

Dates: 23 November–21 December

Strengths: Expansiveness, love of travel and exploration, clear vision, seeking after truth, wide perspectives, flexibility, open-mindedness, optimism, boundless enthusiasm, creativity

Colour: Bright yellow

Crystals: Ruby, turquoise

Incenses: Sage, sandalwood

Planet: Jupiter

Element: Fire

♑ Capricorn

Symbol: The goat

Dates: 22 December–20 January

Ruling angel: Anael (Hanael, Haniel)

Strengths: Wise caution, persistence no matter what the opposition, respecter of tradition and the need to follow tried and tested methods, ambition, self-discipline, prudence in financial affairs

Colour: Indigo, brown

Crystals: Garnet, tiger's eye, titanium aura

Incenses: Hyacinth, myrrh, cedar

Planet: Saturn

Element: Earth

♒ Aquarius

Symbol: The water carrier

Dates: 21 January–18 February

Ruling angel: Gabriel (or Cambiel – see page 113)

Strengths: Idealism, independence, humanitarianism, inventiveness, detachment from swings of emotion or prejudice, unique perspective on world

Colours: Dark blue

Crystals: Amethyst, blue lace agate, any zircon

Incenses: Lemon, rosemary

Planet: Uranus

Element: Air

♓ Pisces

Symbol: The fish

Dates: 19 February–20 March

Ruling angel: Barakiel (Barchiel)

Strengths: Evolved intuitive powers, sympathy and empathy with others, weaving of myths, awareness of hidden factors, ability to merge with surroundings, attunement to alternative spirituality

Colour: White, mauve

Crystals: Coral, fluorite

Incenses: Honeysuckle, sweet grass, lotus

Planet: Uranus

Element: Water

Angels of the months

Each month also has its own guardian angel. The angel of your birth month will offer his protection and virtues, but you can also work with the angel of the current month if you need to draw on his particular strengths. For example, Barakiel, the Angel of February, presides over good luck, so during February he will help anyone who needs a bit of good fortune or the impetus to try new things. February is a dull dark month when we may feel our fortunes are at low ebb, so he is a hard-working angel.

January: Cambiel or Gabriel

Keyword: Inventiveness

Colour: Dark blue

Crystals: Amethyst, blue lace agate, any zircon

Incenses: Lemon, rosemary

January has two angels, being ruled over by Gabriel, the Watcher, angel also of Aquarius, and by Cambiel. Since we have already met Gabriel (see page 61), we will focus on Cambiel here. Cambiel, Bringer of Originality, is the Angel of January and of Aquarius.

Cambiel is Archangel of the night, who nevertheless has an awareness of all the possibilities in the days ahead. He encourages us to become independent, not needing the approval of others, to develop original ideas and to enjoy our uniqueness.

February: Barakiel (Barchiel)

Keyword: Opportunity

Colours: White, mauve

Crystals: Coral, fluorite

Incenses: Honeysuckle, sweet grass, lotus

Barakiel, the Bringer of Fortune, whose name means 'Lightning of God', is the Angel of February and of Pisces.

113

He is an Archangel and one of the Seraphim, and is traditionally invoked by those needing good luck. Barakiel says that what we regret most are the things we never tried. He promises that the love and trust we freely offer others will be returned three times from many sources.

March: Machidiel (Malahidael)

Keyword: Optimism

Colour: Red

Crystals: Carnelian, diamond, Herkimer diamond

Incenses: Cedar, dragon's blood

Machidiel, the Innovator, is the Angel of March and of Aries.

He rises with the spring and brings love, new beginnings and new hopes as the new growth appears in plants and wild animals, and birds produce their young.

April: Asmodel

Keyword: Creativity

Colour: Pink

Crystals: Rose quartz, emerald

Incenses: Rose, apple blossom

Asmodel, the Creator of What is of Worth, is the angel of April and of Taurus.

A high Cherub, Asmodel is an angel of beauty. He presides over beautiful places and artefacts, and encourages all to create beauty, whether through the arts or in our homes or in the way we live our lives.

May: Ambriel (Ambiel)

Keyword: Learning

Colours: Pale yellow, grey

Crystals: Citrine, sapphire

Incenses: Lavender, lemongrass

Ambriel, the Messenger, is the angel of May and of Gemini.

He is from the angelic choir of Thrones, where he is described as a Prince. He brings change and challenge, causing us to question our current direction and to seek new knowledge or the skills we need to fulfil our destiny.

June: Muriel

Keyword: Gentleness

Colour: Silver

Crystals: Moonstone, pearl

Incenses: Lemon balm, jasmine

Muriel, the Healer, whose name means 'Myrrh', is the angel of June and the ruler of Cancer.

He is one of leading Dominion angels, but is nevertheless concerned with nurturing the weak, protection of the home and healing those who are sick, in pain or distressed. He is said to possess a magical carpet on which he gives beautiful dreams. Sometimes Muriel is given female energies.

July: Verchiel (Zerachiel)

Keyword: Pleasure

Colour: Gold

Crystals: Clear crystal quartz, golden topaz

Incenses: Frankincense, orange

Verchiel, the Joy Bringer, is the angel of July and the ruler of Leo.

Another Dominions ruler, Verchiel is an angel of the south and of the sun at its full height and power. His message is that we should be happy and enjoy the present without worrying about the past or future.

August: Hamaliel

Keyword: Perseverance

Colour: Green

Crystals: Jade, opal

Incenses: Patchouli, thyme

Hamaliel, the Perfectionist, is the Angel of August and of Virgo.

He is a leading angel in the order of Virtues. Not the easiest of angels, Hamaliel, an energetic and practical angel, expects us to put our affairs in order, to sort out urgent paperwork and to clear up any backlogs of essential tasks. This wisdom is based on the traditional need to get in the early ripe grain harvest using the long sunny days so we are ready for the winter.

September: Zuriel

Keyword: Idealism

Colour: Light blue

Crystals: Lapis lazuli, blue topaz

Incense: Lemon verbena, vanilla

Zuriel, the Teacher, is the angel of September and the ruler of Libra.

He is a high angel in the order of Principalities. He is known mainly as the angel who prevents humans doing stupid, impulsive things or overreacting (a very hard-working angel). He encourages calm, reasoned thought, compromise and looking at both sides of the question before making a decision.

October: Bariel (Baruel)

Keyword: Understanding

Colour: Burgundy

Crystals: Aquamarine, aqua aura

Incenses: Pine, mint

Bariel or Baruel, the Wise One, is the Angel of October and of Scorpio.

He is both an Archangel and a member of the Virtues. He knows the secrets of the past and frees us from repeating the same mistakes, so we can learn from our personal as well as our family history.

November: Adnachiel (Advachiel)

Keyword: Curiosity

Colour: Bright yellow

Crystals: Ruby, turquoise

Incenses: Sage, sandalwood

Adnachiel, the Voyager, is the Angel of November and of Sagittarius.

He is ruler of the choir of Principalities. He will assist us in any mental discovery, whether through taking courses and examinations or learning a new hobby. He also presides over actual voyages, both holidays and relocations or house moves. He guards us as we travel on journeys long and short.

December: Anael (Hanael/Haniel)

Keyword: Caution

Colour: Indigo, brown

Crystals: Garnet, tiger's eye, titanium aura

Incenses: Hyacinth, myrrh, cedar

Anael, the Protector, is the angel of December and of Capricorn.

He is chief of the choirs of Principalities and of Virtues. We met him in Chapter 3 in his role as Archangel of marriage, children and reconciliation (see page 67), but here he presides over rest and withdrawal from the outer world to inner stillness.

He helps us to wait and to plan so that we will recognise the right moment to move forward in our lives.

Finding the right angel

There is really no need to worry about whether or not you are calling on the right angel. In some cases, the possible choices will overlap, so it will be simple to know which angel to choose. For example, your zodiac angel and the angel of the month of your birth may well be the same. However, because zodiac signs overlap the months, your birth-month angel and your zodiac angel may be different.

For example, if you were born between 23 and 27 November, your month angel and zodiac angel are one and the same – the faithful Adnachiel – because he is both the Sagittarius angel and the angel of November. Your birthday angel is Vehuel. You can call on either of these angels. If you were born on 3 December, you would have three angels. Your month angel would be the lovely Anael, who promises you a lot of happiness in your life just because you were born in his month of December, your zodiac angel would be Adnachiel, and your birthday angel would be Hahaziah. This is not a problem; it simply means that you have an extra 'bonus' angel! You can call on any of these angels by using the appropriate candle colours, crystals and fragrances.

Angels for special occasions

You can use the lists above to work out the best dates for christenings, weddings and even house moves, according to the qualities of the angels and the different dates they bring with them.

For example, my birthday is 8 March, so Machidiel (March) is my month angel, who gives me new hope. Barakiel (Pisces) is my zodiac angel, who brings new opportunities. My birthday angel (ruling the five-day period in which I was born) is Gabamiah, the angel of sacred chanting, song and music, and of those who perform, write or take pleasure in it.

117

Let's say that I'm going to marry Andrew, born on 2 January. His month and zodiac angels are Cambiel (who rules January, his birth month), and Anael, (who rules Capricorn, his sun sign). Cambiel says Andrew is a free-thinker and Anael indicates persistence. Andrew's birthday angel is Nemamiah, defender of the weak – a lively combination!

So at the wedding there would be my three angels, plus the three of my new husband, and all their assorted candle colours and fragrances.

I could also invite the angel who rules the wedding day – or, indeed, to choose a wedding day that fits the theme of the union. Let's say I decide to marry on 20 November. I would invite Mihael (who rules that day), to bring me married love and fidelity. The blessing of children would, I would hope, be grandchildren – and also my children's affection for my new partner.

Similarly, at a birth all the baby's angels plus those of the mother and father will be present – and will come to the child's future birthday celebrations (up to nine angels, quite a host).

So you see you have an almost infinite choice of angelic help and support ready to call on whenever you need it.

9

Angels of the Hours

As you have progressed through this book, you have learned about a number of angels and Archangels who can bring power, protection and harmony into your life. In this chapter I will be introducing angelic forces that will to help you to regain harmony with the natural rhythms of different times of the day and night.

What are angelic hours?

Each hour of the day and night has its own Archangel. These are the same as the Archangels of the seven days of the week, whom we met in Chapter 6. These hours, in combination with the relevant day of the week, offer you the concentrated energies of the ruling Archangel for rituals, contemplation or prayer.

They are also remarkably useful in your daily life. If you have an important phone call to make or a decision to take during the day, you can use the hour of the Archangel who will best further your cause. Equally, at night you can choose the appropriate hour to focus on particular powers you need for the coming day, or perhaps to ease pain or worry that will otherwise keep you awake.

Calculating angelic hours

The system I describe here is a simplified method of calculating angelic hours. There is a much more complicated and very accurate way of doing this. However, this approximation works very well.

All you need to know are the fixed points of time, i.e. the time of sunrise and sunset for each day. (You can find these in a newspaper or in *Old Moore's Almanack* (Foulsham).) You can then calculate the 60-minute segments from sunrise and all the way to sunset, and from sunset all the way to sunrise for each individual day. You will notice from the charts below that Archangels always rule the hour after sunrise on their own day.

The following instructions may sound complicated, but read through them once or twice and then practise calculating the sunrise-to-sunset and sunset-to-sunrise angels for the day ahead. Once you've got the idea, it really is simple.

○ The first hour after sunrise on a Sunday is always Michael's hour. So if sunrise is at 6.13am, it will be Michael's hour till 7.13. Anael's hour will be from 7.13 to 8.13, and so on. Make sure you start at the precise hour and minute of sunrise.

Sunrise to sunset

Hours	Sunday	Monday	Tuesday	Wednesday	Thursday	Friday	Saturday
1	Michael	Gabriel	Samael	Raphael	Sachiel	Anael	Cassiel
2	Anael	Cassiel	Michael	Gabriel	Samael	Raphael	Sachiel
3	Raphael	Sachiel	Anael	Cassiel	Michael	Gabriel	Samael
4	Gabriel	Samael	Raphael	Sachiel	Anael	Cassiel	Michael
5	Cassiel	Michael	Gabriel	Samael	Raphael	Sachiel	Anael
6	Sachiel	Anael	Cassiel	Michael	Gabriel	Samael	Raphael
7	Samael	Raphael	Sachiel	Anael	Cassiel	Michael	Gabriel
8	Michael	Gabriel	Samael	Raphael	Sachiel	Anael	Cassiel
9	Anael	Cassiel	Michael	Gabriel	Samael	Raphael	Sachiel
10	Raphael	Sachiel	Anael	Cassiel	Michael	Gabriel	Samael
11	Gabriel	Samael	Raphael	Sachiel	Anael	Cassiel	Michael
12	Cassiel	Michael	Gabriel	Samael	Raphael	Sachiel	Anael

Sunset to sunrise

Hours	Sunday	Monday	Tuesday	Wednesday	Thursday	Friday	Saturday
1	Sachiel	Anael	Cassiel	Michael	Gabriel	Samael	Raphael
2	Samael	Raphael	Sachiel	Anael	Cassiel	Michael	Gabriel
3	Michael	Gabriel	Samael	Raphael	Sachiel	Aniel	Cassiel
4	Anael	Cassiel	Michael	Gabriel	Samael	Raphael	Sachiel
5	Raphael	Sachiel	Anael	Cassiel	Michael	Gabriel	Samael
6	Gabriel	Samael	Raphael	Sachiel	Anael	Cassiel	Michael
7	Cassiel	Michael	Gabriel	Samael	Raphael	Sachiel	Anael
8	Sachiel	Aniel	Cassiel	Michael	Gabriel	Samael	Raphael
9	Samael	Raphael	Sachiel	Anael	Cassiel	Michael	Gabriel
10	Michael	Gabriel	Samael	Raphael	Sachiel	Anael	Cassiel
11	Anael	Cassiel	Michael	Gabriel	Samael	Raphael	Sachiel
12	Raphael	Sachiel	Anael	Cassiel	Michael	Gabriel	Samael

○ At the height of summer, the days are much longer than the nights, so you will need more than the 12 hours given on the Sunrise to Sunset list on page 120. In this case, go back to the start of the list and continue down it till you hit sunset. Of course, because the nights are shorter than 12 hours, you will not need to use all the hours given on the Sunset to Sunrise list. That's fine.

○ Likewise, in the depths of winter, the nights are much longer than the days. Again, just go back to the start of the Sunset to Sunrise list and continue working down it. You will not use up all of the hours in the Sunrise to Sunset list in winter.

○ Start your sunset period at the precise time of sunset and again work in whole hours, for example, 8.13pm to 9.13pm for the first hour then 9.13pm to 10.13pm for the second.

○ The last hour will generally be incomplete, since it is unlikely that, say, a sunrise at 13 minutes past the hour will be followed by a sunset at 13 minutes past the hour. This does not matter at all.

○ Note that if, say, you are working on the Sunday sunset-to-sunrise period, you go on to the next day's hour angels (that is, the Monday ones) only when you reach the Monday sunrise. For your Sunday early-morning rituals you will still be following the Sunset to Sunrise chart for Sunday, even though in the midnight-to-midnight system that we commonly use, these hours are on Monday morning.

○ If you live in a land where in summer there is virtually no night, during this time you need only ever use the Sunrise to Sunset list, working through the hours from one to 12 and then going back to the beginning again until you hit the next day's sunrise. Then start again with the next day's sunrise list.

To get the hang of it, try to think in angel hours throughout the day. You can practise with children, telling them stories of the different hour angels and, for example, putting them to bed at Michael's hour, after sunset, by the light of his gold candle. Before long, angel hours will be second nature.

If you like, you can calculate a week, a month or even longer ahead and enter the Angel hour names and times for that day in your angel journal or your regular diary (if it is a big one).

The first fifteen minutes of any Angel hour are always the most potent.

If this is too complicated, work with complete hours after the first, so, if Michael's hour on Sunday (sunrise) is 6.13am, go from that till 7am. Then Anael takes over till 8am. Do the same at sunset, so if sunset on Sunday is 8.13pm, start with Sachiel till 9pm then go to Samael till 10pm, and so on.

Using angelic hours for Archangel rituals

When you are working with a particular Archangel, your ritual will be much more powerful if you carry it out at sunrise on his own day. For extra energy and to keep up the flow of power through your life, you might like to repeat the ritual weekly on his day and during his special hours.

You can work with more than one Archangel energy at the same time, choosing the angel to fit your needs. Use the day and hour of the Archangel who represents your most urgent need.

The following are suggestions for simple rituals. You can carry them out in your angel place or outdoors if it is a fine day.

O An Archangel hour ritual can be as simple as lighting the appropriately coloured candle and appropriate incense on the first hour the Archangel rules during sunrise to sunset and speaking your wishes aloud into the flame. Then blow out the candle, sending your request and the light into the cosmos. Leave the incense to burn through. Repeat, if you wish, on the Archangel's first hour in the sunset-to-sunrise period, using fresh materials.

O Another simple ritual is to write your Archangel petition on cream paper with green ink and burn the paper as a taper in the flame of an appropriately coloured candle, speaking the petition aloud as you do so. Place a metal tray beneath the candle so that the paper can burn safely. Bury the ashes. Again, repeat, if you wish, on the Archangel's first hour in the sunset-to-sunrise period, using fresh materials.

O Alternatively, light an appropriately coloured candle, and then light a stick of an appropriate incense from the candle. Place the incense stick in a holder. Facing the candle, speak the name of the Archangel nine times. Then, holding the incense stick in your power hand (the one you write with) write your prayer or wish in incense smoke around the candle three times in spirals as you say it in your mind. Speak the Archangel's name nine more times aloud and then leave the incense and candle to burn through. Again, repeat the ritual during the appropriate after-sunrise hour if you wish.

Whatever ritual you are performing, use your own words to express your needs and remember to include more global issues as well where possible, to bring the good vibes back threefold into your life.

A Michael ritual for a new beginning

Work on a Sunday, the day of the Archangel Michael, and carry out your rite at sunrise, Michael's hour, then again on the fourth hour after sunset, his evening hour on Sunday. You can adapt this ritual to any of the other Archangels by changing the candle colours and incenses, and substituting the appropriate name in the chants and using their sunrise and then their sunset hour on the day of the week they rule.

O At the beginning of the hour, arrange four gold candles in a circle, one at each of the compass points. In the centre, on a small square of cloth, set a clear quartz crystal or Herkimer diamond (Michael crystals).

O Face the candle approximately north (12 o'clock on an imaginary clockface lying flat on the table). Light it and say:

I light this candle to Michael, Archangel of Light, to bring the new beginning I desire.

In your own words, speak briefly about the new beginning you wish for, as though you were talking to a wise father or mother.

O Moving clockwise, light the remaining three candles in turn, repeating the chant and the new beginning you wish for at each candle.

O Half-fill a glass bowl with water and into it drop three pinches of salt (sea salt if possible). With a gold- or silver-coloured paper knife, stir the salt into the water three times, saying:

Michael, Archangel of Light, I ask that you bless this water and make my new beginning swift and easy.

O With the knife, draw an equal-armed cross on the surface of the water and then sprinkle water drops in a clockwise circle round the crystal, saying:

Blessed Michael, may my life be filled with the power of the waters and the earth.

O Light two sticks of an appropriate Michael incense (see page 62). Holding a stick in each hand, turn them together in spirals over the crystal, saying:

Michael, Archangel of Light, let my life be filled with the power of the fire and the winds.

Place the incense sticks in holders at the east and west.

O Now blow out the candles in reverse order of lighting, saying before you extinguish each one:

I thank you, Michael, Archangel of Light, and ask your blessings as I go towards my new beginning.

O Leave the incense to burn through. After carrying out the ritual on the second Michael hour, carry the crystal with you in a small purse as a reminder of the power of Michael.

A Samael and Michael ritual for a new beginning under difficulty

If you are afraid of starting again you can carry out a more powerful version of the ritual above by using two Samael hours on a Sunday, Michael's day. Samael hours are the seventh after sunrise and the second after sunset. For double power, carry out the ritual on both Samael's and Michael's hours in the same day – or use one Archangel's candle colour and the other's incense.

O   Carry out the ritual as above, but on the first Samael sunrise hour light a gold Michael candle and two Samael cinnamon or fern incense sticks.

O   Name both Archangels in the chants and ask them to aid you in your endeavour. When you speak about your new beginning, talk also about your fears, asking that Samael give you the courage to overcome them.

O   Empower one of Michael's crystals, as in the ritual above. If you are carrying out the ritual at Samael's sunset hour as well, put the Michael crystal into a small purse and carry it with you.

O   On the second Samael hour of the day (after sunset), light a red Samael candle and Michael incenses and empower a red garnet or other Samael crystal. At the end of this ritual, add the empowered Samael crystal to your purse.

Angels of time can amplify our own particular energies and help us to overcome fears and challenges. The more you tune into their angelic powers, the more your own innate abilities to cope are activated. We will next work with the lovely moon angels, who bring harmony and help us to link with our own rhythms.

10

Angels of the Moon

Wherever we live, be it in a city or forest, near the ocean or on a plain, we see the moon as she passes overhead, following her continuing monthly cycle of birth, growth, maturity, decline, death and rebirth. Her monthly path mirrors the human life cycle and female hormonal cycle. But for men as well as women the internal energy clock is regulated by the monthly ebbs and flows of the moon. When we swim against that lunar tide, we can become bad-tempered or lethargic.

Archangels of the moon

Archangels of the moon are invariably gentle. They bring us into harmony with the natural ebbs and flows of our spiritual, mental and physical energies. They are very calming if you live a stressful life and are all very protective of children and women.

Gabriel

Gabriel is the supreme Archangel of the Moon. You can call on him whenever you need the moon's intuitive energies, especially on his moon day, the fifth after the new moon (the new moon is marked as a solid black circle in diaries and almanacs). Count the new moon day as day 1. Gabriel's moon day will bring new hope for the coming month.

As I have already said, some people regard Gabriel as having a more female focus – for more information see page 61.

Ofaniel (Ofanil)

Ofaniel is another important Archangel of the Moon, watching over the lunar wheel as it turns each month. He has been described as having 100 pairs of silver wings and being able to see everywhere at once. He stands near the throne of God and regulates the stars as the wheel of the year brings each new constellation into focus. He is sometimes linked with Sandalaphon (see page 73). Picture him radiating silver light and holding a huge wheel of stars.

The daily moon angels

Each day of the moon cycle has its own angel, on whom we can call and who will help us to attune with the natural rhythms of the world, even if we live and work in tall buildings.

Each individual moon angel has a subtle energy. Those waxing (or increasing) moon angels who rule the days up to and including the full moon (days 3–15) gradually increase our power and energy flow. Day 15 and 16 are peaks of lunar angel power, and thereafter, on days 17–29, the waning or (decreasing) moon angels gently guide us towards the end of the cycle. They can help us to shed what we no longer want in our life and to conserve our energies where possible. The angels of days 1 and 2 sit at the centre of the cosmic seesaw and provide the balance. With their help, we reflect on the past and look to the future as we prepare to start the journey through the moon cycle again.

You might wonder if it's worth the effort of working out which moon angel day it is. In fact this is easy. You can buy ready-marked moon calendars and diaries (your current one may already have the moon days). You can also find out on-line or by checking the weather section of some newspapers.

The cycle from new moon to new moon lasts 29.5 days. It takes just over 27 days for the moon to complete its orbit round the Earth. For this reason moon phases vary slightly in length from month to month. The angelic moon calendar works on 28 angels for 28 days. If a cycle lasts for 29 days, you just use the angel of day 28 twice.

Moonlight increases from the right, so the moon is first seen as crescent with points facing left. As the light continues to increase from the right, the moon waxes until full moon. Thereafter, the light disappears from the right until only a sliver-thin crescent remains on the left, with the points facing right.

If you watch the moon in the sky over two or three months, you will become aware of how it rises over particular landmarks at different times in the cycle. In the summer, when I live in my caravan in a field with no artificial light, I can see the moon wheeling around. I can paddle through the moonlight path on the days leading up to the full moon and feel the angels dancing in the waves on the usually deserted beach.

Gradually, as you connect with the angels of the moon, your body and mind will naturally harmonise with the monthly rhythms and you will feel more in tune with yourself, calmer and happier (and PMS improves rapidly).

The 28 angels of the moon

1 Geniel	2 Enediel	3 Anixiel	4 Azariel
5 Gabriel	6 Dirachiel	7 Scheliel	8 Amnediel
9 Barbiel	10 Ardifiel	11 Neciel	12 Abdizuel
13 Jazariel	14 Ergediel	15 Atliel	16 Azeruel
17 Adriel	18 Egibiel	19 Amutiel	20 Kyriel
21 Bethnael	22 Geliel	23 Requiel	24 Abrimael
25 Aziel	26 Tagriel	27 Atheniel	28 Anixiel

Moon angels and lunar phases

Each of the moon phases listed below lasts between two and four days, depending on the individual month. Don't worry if you are a day out, as the energies do overlap. If in doubt, check on what is happening in the sky with the moon.

Moon angels tend to have a female energy, some strikingly so, especially those early and late in the lunar cycle.

New moon: days 1, 2 and 3 Geniel, Enediel and Anixiel

The new (or dark) moon rises at dawn and sets at dusk. Because the sun and moon are in the same part of the sky, the sunlight obscures the moon in the day. At night, the moon is on the other side of the earth with the sun, and you will see nothing during this period.

Day 1 is significant as a signature or key day, and is good for meditating and attuning the energies of mind, body and soul with the natural lunar cycles.

Ask the angels of these days for help with formulating new plans, assessing what has gone before and keeping secrets. This is a time when you stand poised for the new month and so can allow ideas to germinate.

When playing their lunar role (you will meet them with other functions and appearances) new-moon angels are seen as black shadowy forms with pale silver wings and halo.

In some months the crescent can appear on day 3, Anixiel's day. If so, work with Anixiel and Azariel and use Azariel again on day 4. In this case you can merge the two energies of new and crescent moon.

Crescent moon: days 4, 5, 6 and 7
Azariel, Gabriel, Dirachiel and Scheliel

The crescent moon rises mid-morning and sets some time after sunset. The moon can be seen on a clear day from moonrise to moonset.

Ask the angels of these days for help with new beginnings and setting plans in motion. They also preside over matters concerning animals and small children, optimism and new love.

With the exception of Gabriel, crescent-moon angels have crescent-shaped haloes and a soft shimmering light all round them. They are very delicate and feminine.

First quarter or waxing: days 8, 9, 10 and 11
Amnediel, Barbiel, Ardifiel and Neciel

The waxing moon rises at about noon and sets at about midnight. The moon can be seen from rise to set.

Ask the angels of these days for improved health, good luck, courage and help with finances. Day 8 is very good for healing. Day 10 is especially good for visions and spiritual insights.

Waxing moon angels are surrounded by radiant silver moonbeams and have glowing golden wings. They are also feminine in energy.

The gibbous (bulging, almost full) moon: days 12, 13 and 14
Abdizuel, Jazeriel and Ergediel

The gibbous moon rises in the middle of the afternoon and sets before dawn the next day. She can be seen from soon after rising until she sets. She is easily recognisable by the bulge on one side.

Ask the angels of these days for increased power or increasing commitment in love, also for patience and for the relief of long-standing illnesses and problems. Days 13 and 14 are good for all purification and cleansing rites (a bit like weeding a garden to allow new flowers to grow).

The angels of this moon wear flowing robes of silver and gold and have long, white-gold, flowing hair.

The full moon: days 15, 16 and 17
Atliel, Azeruel and Adriel

The full moon rises at sunset and sets at sunrise, so there is sometimes a brief period when both sun and full moon are in the sky together – amazing energy. Strictly speaking, 'full moon' refers only to day 15, when the moon is completely full, but this moon's effects do linger, for example in extremes of tides.

Day 15, like day 1, is good for meditation and attuning with the energies of the moon cycle, as well as channelling wisdom from the full-moon angel or from one of the lunar Archangels.

Ask the angels of these days to initiate sudden or dramatic change or give a surge of power. They preside over the consummation of love; healing; prophecy; all matters concerning women, including conception and motherhood; the granting of small miracles; artistic and creative success; and all legal matters.

These are glorious, silver and gold angels, studded with stars and with huge, full, starry haloes.

The disseminating (or waning) moon: days 18, 19, 20 and 21
Egibiel, Amutiel, Kyriel and Bethnael

The full moon is shrinking and rises now in mid-evening, setting in the middle of the next morning, and is visible for much of the time.

Ask the angels of the waning moon for protection of home, self and loved ones, for help with banishing bad habits, phobias and fears, for ending a long-standing destructive or abusive relationship, for relieving acute pain and fighting viruses, and for leaving behind a past that holds you back from happiness.

These are mature, female angels, with pure white robes and pale, shimmering, blue haloes and wings.

The waning half-moon (or last-quarter moon): days 22, 23, 24
and 25:   Geliel, Requiel, Abrimael and Aziel

This moon rises at about midnight and sets around midday the next day. She is visible for the whole time she is in the sky.

Day 23 is for healing, and day 25 for all women's prayers and needs.

Ask the angels of the waning half-moon for safety while travelling, especially at night; for protection from phantoms, nightmares and fears that come in the night; for the reduction of major debts; for the welfare of older people; for mending quarrels; for avoiding intrusion into privacy; for peaceful divorce; and for relieving stress.

These angels are misty, but their wings and haloes still shimmer silver and gold. They are dark-haired and female in their energy.

The balsamic (or waning crescent) moon: days 26, 27, 28 (and 29)
Tagriel, Atheniel and Anixiel

The balsamic moon rises before dawn (after the midnight of its day) and sets mid-afternoon on the following day. She is best seen in the eastern sky at dawn and in the very early morning.

Ask the angels of the waning crescent for quiet sleep if you are an insomniac, for peace of mind if you have been anxious or depressed, for protection from crime and harm, for the easing of addictions, for saying goodbye gently and for finding what is lost or has been stolen. Angelic protection is strongest on these three (or four) days.

These angels are almost transparent, with a single star on their headdress and silver-grey hair. They are female in type and are slow in their movements.

Working with the moon angels

Moon angels are concerned with our subconscious mind, with our feelings, insights and intuitions, and with, as I have said, our natural rhythms – not only of the body but also of the mind and spirit.

Getting to know the moon angels can take a long time, as there are 28 of them, but it is well worthwhile and you need not hurry. At first you may become aware of the marker-point angels. For example, when the crescent moon first appears in the sky, around the third day of the cycle, Anixiel rules; when the moon reaches full, on the 15th day, it is the time of Atliel. Allow images and impressions of each moon angel to come into your mind. The following are a few suggestions of ways to do this.

O Keep a page for each lunar angel in your angel diary. Write down what happens and, most importantly, what you feel on each day of the moon cycle. You will soon detect patterns.

O Call on the moon angel of the night by reciting the name nine times while looking at the moon in the sky, preferably outdoors. If it is cloudy or rises when you are asleep, gaze into a clear glass bowl of water on which you have set silver floating candles.

O Burn a lunar incense such as eucalyptus, jasmine, lily, myrrh, lilac or lemon. Rose is used for both the moon angels and angels of love, such as Anael, Archangel of Friday.

O You can empower anything made of silver, such as an earring, with the qualities of a particular moon phase. Spiral the smoke from a moon-incense stick (see above) over the item continuously as you recite in turn all the names of the angels of the lunar phase nine times. Then make your wish nine times silently as you hold the silver object towards the moon (or over a silver floating candle in a bowl of water – see above – if it is cloudy or before moonrise). Leave the item on a window ledge or other place exposed to the night sky throughout all the nights of the moon phase.

O You can empower a moon crystal such as aquamarine, aqua aura, moonstone, milky quartz, opal aura, opals, pearls or selenite in the same way.

O Choose one of the nights in the relevant moon period (for example, the crescent moon for new love) and melt a silver or beeswax candle (a wax-based rather than a paraffin-based church-type one, as the latter do not melt in a pool) on a metal tray when the moon is (or should be) visible in the sky. When the wax has melted and slightly solidified, use a knife or small silver screwdriver to engrave the names of the moon angels of your chosen phase in it. Allow the wax to set and then cut out a circle containing the names. Leave it on the window ledge till the moon phase ends, when you should wrap it in a white cloth and keep it as a talisman until it crumbles.

As you get to know the different angels, you need only sit quietly on their night looking at the moon or a silver candle, and say their name. If you hear a message in your mind from the angel, record it. Over time, you may find that your moon' angels are guiding you towards a wise path.

11

Female Angels

We do not hear much about female angels, partly because, as I explained earlier, angels are androgynous, neither male nor female. This is because they are not human. However, we tend to perceive and describe them in a human form because this is what we can relate to. But this is only part of the story. The main reason for the lack of information about female angels is that early angelologists operated within an a male-focused society. Angels were traditionally regarded as warriors against those who did not believe in the one true faith (although the definition of that one true faith varied). Thus Archangel Michael is depicted in red and gold with a shining sword, the ideal golden warrior, and Archangel Camael, whose planet is Mars, in green and red armour.

Women were viewed by the early Church leaders with great suspicion because of the sins of Eve, who was entirely blamed for the fall of humankind and the loss of Paradise. Indeed, the mighty Watcher angels were said to have likewise fallen from grace because they were tempted by and consorted with mortal women. Rarely, a pre-Christian goddess became absorbed into Christian theology in the form of an angel – this happened to Iris (see pages 10 and 96), who was originally an Ancient Greek rainbow goddess. More often, however, the ancient goddesses were demonised.

Nevertheless, positive images of female angels do exist in history. In some of Michelangelo's paintings, angels are shown as beautiful, graceful and feminine. A painting by Edward Hughes, dating from the beginning of the 1900s, shows a dark, winged, female angel in the deep blue of the night. The painting is called *Night and her Train*. A trail of small, blue, winged angels encircle her in the night sky. My own favourite depiction of a female angel is *The Angel of Death*, by Carlos Schwabe, a painter of the same period. This shows the death angel as a beautiful, green-winged woman, dressed in jade and surrounded by green light. She is set against the white snow of a winter cemetery and is encouraging a frightened man to leave his grave so she may take him to heaven.

But it was not until the rise of feminism in the 1970s, and the return to a more balanced view of spirituality, with women priests being ordained in many parts of the world, that female angels came back into general awareness.

The powerful female angels

Female angels often appear to women, and a number of them are associated with women, children, fertility or childbirth, but they are also very important for men in their nurturing role.

The following female angels are among the best-known and most potent. Visualise them however you like. Often they will come when you are sad, afraid or alone. Then their face may suddenly resemble that of a deceased and much-loved grandmother or a living mother, sister or best friend far away, whose presence we crave at a time of crisis.

Sophia, angel of wisdom

Sophia means 'wisdom' in Greek, and the angel Sophia represents wisdom in the Old Testament. In the Hebrew tradition, Sophia is considered to have been with God from the beginning of creation. She became Saint Sophia, or Holy Sophia, Mother Russia, much beloved in the Russian and Greek Orthodox churches. In modern female spirituality she is regarded as one of two supreme female angels (the other being Shekinah).

Shekinah, queen of the angels

Shekinah, called the Queen of Angels in the Jewish mystical system, is the angel who brings freedom to those who are oppressed or who imprison themselves through fear. At dusk on Friday evenings, she lights the Sabbath candles in Jewish homes, through the hands of the mother or eldest daughter.

Shekinah is an aspect of the feminine side of God. Her love enters women when they make love with their true mate, and she attends all marriages and informal unions. She encourages humanity towards perfection, staying close to them to heal their sorrows and encourage them through difficult times. She is also an angel of truth, justice and integrity.

The angel (or golden lady) clothed in the sun

In the Book of Revelations, this angel is described as 'clothed with the sun, and the moon under her feet, and upon her head a crown of 12 stars'. She is pregnant and will assist all who seek a child, whether by birth or through adoption or fostering. She also protects those who care for, teach or nurse other people's children, or who look after any family members who are sick, disabled or old. She is sometimes linked with the Virgin Mary.

Iris, angel of the rainbow

Iris has rainbow wings and carries a beautifully formed purple and yellow iris and a golden lily. She comforts bereaved husbands, and sorrowing sons and daughters who have lost a mother, as well as all who feel alone and need comfort. She also unites estranged family and lovers.

Other female angels

The following female angels are slightly less well known, and information about them is sparser. However, their energies are nonetheless relevant to women's lives.

Anhita

She ensures that the earth remains fruitful and brings fertility to all life. She also protects those who care for the earth and fight against pollution.

Ardousta

Called Lady of the Living Waters, she assists women to become pregnant, by natural or artificially assisted means, and to have an easy labour. She ensures that breast milk will flow freely and helps all mothers to bond with their children.

Armait

Armait brings truth, goodness and wisdom, and endeavours to maintain peace and harmony among nations and families alike.

Armisael

She is the angel who protects the unborn in the womb. She will assist with all births, whether natural or involving medical intervention. She also aids conception.

Aruru

A Middle-Eastern angel messenger who assisted in the creation of humans from clay, she can be called upon for all creative ventures. She assists self-employed women and any who work from home.

Barbelo (Barbelu)

Called Perfect in Glory, she brings abundance and helps women to claim their own power, as well as good working and childcare conditions. She also brings out talents and encourages us to be true, not least to ourselves. Work with this angel for a faithful marriage.

Bath Kol (Bath Qol)

Called the Daughter of the Voice, she cried out in vain to try to stop Cain killing his brother Abel. Her symbol is the white dove, and she is the peacemaker. She visits those who are unfairly imprisoned – be it by an unjust regime, by disability or by fear – or who are exiled and far from home. She encourages honest communication and also enhances prophecy, giving insights into the future.

Derdekea

Called Supreme Mother, she lives on earth in order to help humans attain perfection. She is the protectress of homes, families, land and property.

Eloa

A New Testament angel of compassion, she was born from a tear shed by Jesus in the Garden of Gethsemane before his arrest. She guards all who have difficult or dangerous jobs or are starting again with a new life, career or love.

Faith, Hope and Charity

These three sisters are the daughters of Sophia. Together they represent the triple virtues of believing in what is right and of worth, knowing that it is possible to attain our dreams if we try hard enough, and encouraging generosity and sharing of good fortune with others. You can invoke all three at once as a single invocation, since they invariably appear and act together.

Ouestucati

Called the Lady of the Pure Hands, she carries with her gentle breezes of warm seas. She is protectress of all animals and birds, as well as of the young, and an uplifter in times of doubt or hardship.

Sekel (Seket)

She is an Egyptian angel who brings courage to women, especially those who, in the modern world, are trying to combine home and career. She is a healing angel and will help all who call on her, especially for the easing of addictions and depression.

Sereda

Often called Mother Sereda, she is best invoked on a Wednesday, her day. This is another healing angel. The Divine Washerwoman, she cleanses all and washes away sorrow, evil and divisions between different peoples and ideologies.

Using female angelic energy

It has been said that love can take the form of an angel and fly to us when we feel most isolated. When you work with the angels above, you may feel a feather-light touch or a sense of being held and cherished.

Female angel crystals include rose quartz, purple or green fluorite, green or pink tourmaline, peach or green aventurine, jade, chrysoprase, sugilite (purple and quite expensive but very beautiful), opal or angel aura, amethyst, pink calcite, pink or green opal, moonstones and milk or snow quartz. Alternatively, use tiny rose quartz or amethyst crystal angels at each of the four main directions to enclose your candle, and incense.

Female angel fragrances include carnation, geranium, hyacinth, lilac, lavender, lily, lily of the valley, mimosa and rose.

A ritual to make a request of a female angel

Work after dusk, in your angel place. For this ritual you will be invoking all four of the most powerful female angels. You will also be invoking a fifth, from the list of other angels – choose one whose concerns most nearly match your own.

❍ Light a beeswax candle and put it in the middle of your working surface. (Bees and beeswax were once sacred to the ancient Mother Goddess, and in Christian times they are blessed by the Virgin Mary and her mother, St Anne.)

❍ Light an incense stick from the candle, and set it to the right or east of the candle as you face north.

❍ Into a small dish, pour a little cologne in one of the above fragrances, or some water to which a few drops of concentrated floral perfume have been added. Place this to the left or west of the candle as you face north – not too close as perfume is flammable.

❍ Working clockwise, encircle the candle, incense, and dish of fragrance with small pink and purple glass nuggets or tiny female angel crystals. You can mix the crystals. For each crystal, name what you seek from the angel you are invoking.

❍ Take the dish of perfume in your power hand (the one you write with) and face the candle.

❍ With your other hand, anoint the centre of your hairline, the centre of your brow, the centre of your throat and your wrist pulse points (left and right) – set the dish down to do this. As you touch each of the five points, say softly three times:

Iris, Sophia, Shekinah, Golden Lady Clothed in the Sun,
(and then the name of the angel you have chosen).

137

○ Face the candle and name your request, then once again say the five angel names three times.

○ Blow out the candle and again repeat the five names, this time so softly they can scarcely be heard.

○ When the incense is burned through replace it with a fresh unlighted stick. Leave the candle, new incense and dish of perfume surrounded by the crystals for 24 hours after the ritual.

○ If possible, replace all these items with a fragrant pot plant.

Men as well as women can benefit from these softer but nevertheless potent female angelic forces. Spend time connecting with them and, as I have found, angel study and practice becomes personal and comforting as well as uplifting.

12

Angels Everywhere

There is no room to write any more about angels in this book, yet stories still come. Last night, for example I watched a television programme about a UK TV presenter, Caron Keating, who bravely fought against cancer but lost. After her death, her husband said she had become the family guardian angel, and white feathers would flutter down when he was drinking coffee – in places where there were no birds. Caron's mother, Gloria Hunniford, a well-known UK television presenter herself, recounted how, after Caron's death, she was mediating in a dispute between Reuben, one of Caron's children, and a cousin. Gloria felt she had handled the situation well, as Caron would have wanted. Then a tiny white feather fluttered down as confirmation.

I am reminded of the teachings of Emanuel Swedenborg, of whom I spoke on page 12. He believed that all people have the potential to become angels, whatever their religion (and, I would argue, even if they have no religious faith). If they choose the path of virtue, he said, they can continue on an angelic path after death. Maybe we don't actually become winged beings with golden haloes, but the more we welcome and experience angelic energies into our lives, the more our own spiritual potential increases.

Angels don't take away the need to organise our own lives. Rather, they give us the strength to follow our chosen life path – and sometimes to change that life path if it is not leading anywhere. Above all, angels are there when we are sad or frightened and will enfold us in love and approval, giving us the will to face the future with optimism and determination.

You may decide to read more about the angels I have described or to trust yourself to see and interact with angels in your own unique way. There are no angel experts, except maybe young children. In my experience, the more you discover about angels, the more you find there is to learn.

I am finishing this book as Christmas ends, surrounded by wilting holly and discarded Christmas wrappings. Having put life on hold for a few glorious days with my children, my gall stones and bank balance are now reminding me that the everyday world is waiting in the wings. Tomorrow I will call on my household angel, who has kept everyone harmonious over Christmas and ensured the roast potatoes were properly browned for the feast. My overworked guardian angel helpfully tries to minimise the pile of must-do-yesterday lists. Dear Archangel Cassiel reassures me that I completed my tax returns last year with six hours to spare and can do so again, once I have sorted the 12 boxes of receipts.

But for tonight I will sit by my magical glowing fairylights, looking at the golden-winged angel on top of the Christmas tree, and know that the angels aren't a million miles away across the universe, but are here in the heart of my family.

Index

Other books by Cassandra Eason

Cassandra's books are available from all good bookshops or direct from www.foulsham.com. You can also visit her website at www.cassandraeason.co.uk.

Cassandra Eason's Complete Book of Spells (0-572-03001-0)
Cassandra Eason's Modern Book of Dream Interpretation (0-572-03081-9)
Chakra Power for Healing and Harmony (0-572-02749-4)
Contact Your Spirit Guides to Enrich Your Life (0-572-03128-9)
Crystal Healing (0-572-02735-4)
Crystals Talk to the Woman Within (0-572-02613-7)
Discover Your Past Lives (0-572-02198-4)
Every Woman a Witch (0-572-02223-9)
Fragrant Magic (0-572-02939-X)
I Ching Divination for Today's Woman (0-572-01895-9)
Magic Spells for a Happy Life (0-572-02827-X)
Practical Guide to Witchcraft and Magick Spells (0-572-02704-4)
Psychic Protection (0-572-02645-5)
Runes Talk to the Woman Within (0-572-02612-9)
Smudging and Incense-burning (0-572-02737-0)
Tarot Talks to the Woman Within (0-572-02614-5)